国家级一流本科专业建设配套教材

商务英语写作实用教程

BUSINESS ENGLISH WRITING: A PRACTICAL COURSE

易文静 万菁婧 徐静

编著

U0360069

清华大学出版社

北京

内 容 简 介

本书充分整合了与商务英语写作相关的理论和实践知识，专为非英语母语的学习者量身打造，内容涵盖商务英语写作基础与技巧、特定商务词汇和表达方式、常见商务文体格式及跨文化沟通技巧。教材按照难易程度划分为基础（写作过程、语调和读者分析等）、进阶（构建主旨句、视觉辅助工具的使用、列表和项目符号的应用等）和高级（求职、公关、市场营销等特殊领域写作的技巧）三个层次，辅以翔实的例子和基于理论的解释。书中还精选了实际商务写作练习，包括商务邮件、备忘录、报告等多种商务文体，使学习者真正做到理论与实践相结合，为职场成功奠定坚实的写作基础。本书配有 PPT 课件，读者可登录 www.tsinghuaelt.com 下载使用。

本书适合英语类专业（尤其是商务英语专业）及管理学相关专业的本科生和研究生使用，也适合企业员工使用，尤其是需要与国外同事、客户或合作伙伴进行书面沟通的员工。

图书在版编目（CIP）数据

商务英语写作实用教程 / 易文静，万菁婧，徐静编著 . —北京：清华大学出版社，2024.12
国家级一流本科专业建设配套教材
ISBN 978-7-302-66398-0

Ⅰ．①商…　Ⅱ．①易…　②万…　③徐…　Ⅲ．①商务—英语—写作—高等学校—教材　Ⅳ．①F7

中国国家版本馆 CIP 数据核字 (2024) 第 111462 号

责任编辑：刘　艳
封面设计：李伯骥
责任校对：王荣静
责任印制：杨　艳

出版发行：清华大学出版社
　　　　　网　　　址：https://www.tup.com.cn, https://www.wqxuetang.com
　　　　　地　　　址：北京清华大学学研大厦 A 座　　　邮　　编：100084
　　　　　社 总 机：010-83470000　　　　　　　　　邮　　购：010-62786544
　　　　　投稿与读者服务：010-62776969, c-service@tup.tsinghua.edu.cn
　　　　　质量反馈：010-62772015, zhiliang@tup.tsinghua.edu.cn
印 装 者：三河市龙大印装有限公司
经　　销：全国新华书店
开　　本：185mm×260mm　　　印　　张：16.75　　　字　　数：303 千字
版　　次：2024 年 12 月第 1 版　　　　　　　印　　次：2024 年 12 月第 1 次印刷
定　　价：69.00 元

产品编号：106470-01

前 言

随着全球化进程的不断加速，商务英语写作已经成为许多职场人士必不可少的技能，但如何有效、准确且具有说服力地书写商务英语文件仍然是许多人面临的挑战。基于此，本书旨在帮助读者掌握商务英语写作的基本技能。无论您是初学者还是想进一步提高自己的商务英语写作能力，本书都可以提供全面的指导，因为本书涵盖了从基本写作原则到高级商务写作策略的所有内容。

本教材主要特色如下：

1. 实用导向：深入讲解商务英语写作的基本理论与实践，强调知识在真实工作环境中的应用，提升学生的职场适应能力。

2. 内容全面：涵盖基本写作原则和特定商务领域（如公关、市场营销、人力资源、求职等）内容，培养学生在各类商务场景中的写作能力。

3. 强调跨文化理解：专为非英语母语者设计，侧重跨文化沟通技巧并提供理论指导，增强学生的文化敏感性，拓宽其国际视野。

4. 内容循序渐近：章节内容由浅入深，从基础知识到特殊主题，系统性强，易于学习和掌握。

5. 实战演练：包含丰富实例、练习和任务，通过实际写作活动巩固学习成果，提高学生的实战能力和职场竞争力。

6. 教学多样化：结合书本、课堂练习和互动活动，提供多元化学习体验，满足不同学生的个性化需求。

7. 灵活适用：既适合课堂教学，也适合个人自学，满足多样化的学习需求，是一本适合各类学习者和教育场景的商务英语写作指南。

以上特色使本书成为一本全面、实用、灵活的商务英语写作指南，适合英语类专业（尤其是商务英语专业）及管理学相关专业的本科生和研究生。本书也适合企业员工使用，尤其是需要与国外同事、客户或合作伙伴进行书面沟通的员工。

本书共七个单元，每个单元专注于不同方面的商务英语写作。第1单元介绍课程概览和课程目标，强调商务英语写作的重要性及独特特征，如正式性与精确性；第2单元探讨写作过程、写作目的、语调和风格及读者的重要性；第3单元讨论如何突出

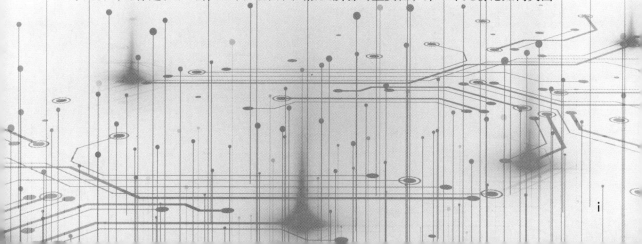

读者的好处、积极表达、使用包容性语言、保持专业而对话式的语言、在商务写作中使用强调和减弱强调等内容；第 4 单元包含商务写作的组织、主旨句的构建、视觉辅助工具的使用、列表和项目符号的运用；第 5 单元探讨商业词汇的重要性、习语表达的使用，以及不同商务情境下的短语运用；第 6 单元详细介绍商务电子邮件、商务信函、备忘录、商务报告、商务提案的写作方法；第 7 单元涵盖求职、社交媒体、公关、营销等特殊领域的写作策略和技巧。

　　本书采用结构化方法，从基础知识开始，逐渐深入，帮助学生提高其商务英语写作能力。每个单元都包括实际示例、练习和任务，以帮助学生巩固所学内容。我们鼓励学生积极参与，勤加练习，并将所学应用于实际工作中。

　　本书由江西师范大学国际教育学院资助，易文静主编，万菁婧和徐静参与编写。在编写过程中，我们参阅和借鉴了有关著作及资料，在此向相关作者深表谢意。由于水平和时间有限，书中难免有疏漏之处，敬请广大专家和读者批评指正。

编者

2024 年 11 月

Contents

Unit 3

Business Writing Skills

Unit 4

Business Writing Strategies

Unit 5

Business Vocabulary and Expressions

Unit 6

Business Writing Formats

Unit 7

Special Topics

Unit 1

Introduction

1.1

Overview of the Course

Business English Writing is a specialized course designed for students majoring in Business English and individuals engaged in English-mediated international transactions, especially within regions where English is spoken as a second language (L2). This comprehensive program is dedicated to enhancing students' proficiency in writing across a wide range of business contexts, including but not limited to e-mails, letters, memos, reports, proposals, and content for social media, public relations, marketing, and human resources.

At the heart of this course lie the foundational principles of the writing process. Students will delve into understanding the objectives behind their writing tasks, selecting an appropriate tone and style, accurately identifying their target audience, and constructing compelling thesis statements. Additionally, the curriculum covers the vital aspects of business writing skills, expanding students' business vocabulary, and introducing idiomatic expressions and phrases apt for various business scenarios.

A key feature of this course is its emphasis on practical writing strategies. Participants will learn how to structure their documents effectively, incorporate visual aids to enhance their messages, and refine their drafts through rigorous editing and proofreading exercises. Moreover, the course offers ample opportunities for students to apply their learning in real-world business situations, fostering hands-on experience through writing practice and personalized feedback.

Business English Writing sets out with the goal of molding students into proficient communicators within the professional business milieu. It aims to bolster their confidence and competence in writing, ensuring that they are well-equipped to navigate the complexities of business communication. By the end of the course, students are expected to master the essential skills and knowledge indispensable for excelling in diverse business writing tasks.

1.2
Course Objectives

The course objectives for Business English Writing are:

- Developing proficiency in writing for various business situations, such as e-mails, letters, memos, reports, proposals, and content for social media, public relations, marketing, and human resources;

- Understanding the purpose of writing in a business context, including choosing the appropriate tone and style, identifying the audience, and crafting a strong thesis statement;

- Expanding business vocabulary and acquiring idiomatic expressions and phrases for different business situations;

- Developing strategies for organizing writing, using visual aids, and editing and proofreading written works;

- Practicing writing in different business contexts and receiving feedback on writing skills;

- Understanding how to write for specific business audiences, such as employees, customers, and stakeholders;

- Developing critical thinking and analytical skills necessary for effective business writing;

- Enhancing cross-cultural communication skills by understanding cultural differences that impact business communication;

- Building confidence in communicating effectively in a professional business setting in written and oral communication.

Overall, these objectives aim to equip students with the necessary skills and knowledge to communicate effectively in a business setting, helping them become competent and confident writers.

1.3
Importance of Business English Writing

Business English writing is important nowadays for several reasons.

1.3.1 Professionalism

Effective communication is essential in any professional setting, and business writing is no exception. Business English writing ensures that the tone, structure, and content of written communication are professional, appropriate, and effective.

1.3.2 Efficiency

Well-written business documents can save time and resources. Clear and concise communication helps ensure that all parties involved understand the messages and can act accordingly, leading to better decision-making and increased productivity.

1.3.3 Reputation

Good business writing reflects positively on an individual, an organization, or a brand. Conversely, poor writing skills can damage an organization's reputation, causing a loss of trust and credibility.

1.3.4 Cross-Cultural Communication

In today's global business environment, it is essential to be able to communicate effectively with people from different cultures. Business English writing provides students with the tools and skills to communicate with international colleagues and clients in the future, avoiding misunderstandings that can arise from cultural differences.

1.3.5 Career Advancement

Strong writing skills can help individuals advance in their careers. Employers value employees who can write clearly and effectively, and excellent writing skills can open up new job opportunities and lead to higher salaries.

Overall, business English writing is a critical skill that can enhance an individual's professional and personal life. Effective communication is the cornerstone of business success, and good writing skills are essential for anyone looking to succeed in the business world.

1.4
Distinctive Features of Business English Writing

Business English writing stands out due to its unique characteristics tailored to the professional environment. This section delves into the distinctive features of business English writing that set it apart from general English writing, focusing on the precision, clarity, and efficiency required in business communication.

1.4.1 Formality and Precision

Business English writing often requires a higher degree of formality compared with general English writing. This includes the use of specific jargon and formal expressions and avoiding colloquial language. Precision is also key, as clarity in conveying exact meanings is crucial in business transactions and communication.

1.4.2 Structured Format and Purpose-Driven Writing

Business documents are typically more structured. They often follow a specific format depending on the type of the document—a report, memo, e-mail, or proposal. Each type serves a specific purpose and thus, the writing style adapts to meet the objective, whether it's to inform, persuade, request, or record.

1.4.3 Conciseness and Clarity

In business writing, conveying messages in a concise and clear manner is valued. This is because business professionals often have limited time; therefore, getting the message across effectively in the shortest possible way is crucial. This doesn't mean oversimplification, but rather, presenting ideas in a direct and unambiguous manner.

1.4.4 Tone Adaptability

The tone in business English writing varies greatly depending on the context, audience, and purpose. For example, a business proposal to a new client may have a more persuasive and formal tone compared with an internal e-mail to colleagues, which might be more casual yet still professional.

1.4.5 Cultural Sensitivity

Given the global nature of business, writing in a culturally sensitive manner is essential. This includes understanding and respecting cultural differences in communication styles and business etiquette, which can vary widely from one region to another.

1.4.6 Focusing on Relationship Building

Unlike general English, business English often entails building and maintaining professional relationships. Therefore, the language used may include elements of diplomacy, politeness, and a degree of personalization, aiming to establish trust and rapport.

1.4.7 Use of Persuasive Language

In many business writing scenarios, especially in marketing, sales, and proposals, persuasive language is a key feature. This involves using language that can influence and convince the reader or recipient to take a certain course of action.

1.4.8 Adaptability to Digital Platforms

With the rise of digital communication, business English writing has adapted to various platforms like e-mails, social media, and professional networking sites. Each platform may require different styles and lengths of writing.

Class Activity 1: *Written communication plays a crucial role in various aspects of business interactions. Have a discussion with your classmates and give some examples that highlight the significance of written communication.*

Class Activity 2: *Clear and effective writing plays a significant role in enhancing credibility and professionalism in various business contexts. Read the following* *examples and then discuss their roles with your classmates.*

> **Example 1:** Dear Mr. Smith, I hope this e-mail finds you well. I would like to discuss the upcoming project and the timeline for its execution. Could we schedule a brief call to go over the details?
>
> **Example 2:** Hey Smith, need 2 talk bout proj. whn free?
>
> **Example 3:** A quarterly sales report with data, analysis, and insights, using headings and bullet points for clarity.
>
> **Example 4:** A sales report with scattered information, unclear charts, and missing context.
>
> **Example 5:** Our proposal outlines a tailored strategy to boost your online presence and increase customer engagement.
>
> **Example 6:** We can help make u popular online. Let us know if interested.
>
> **Example 7:** A financial consulting firm's website with clear descriptions of services and expertise.
>
> **Example 8:** A website with vague descriptions and grammar errors.
>
> **Example 9:** Experience luxury and comfort with our premium travel packages.
>
> **Example 10:** You'll like our trips; they're good.
>
> **Example 11:** An internal memo detailing a new company policy with reasons and implications.
>
> **Example 12:** An unclear memo leaving employees confused about policy changes.
>
> **Example 13:** I apologize for the inconvenience. Let me assist you in resolving this issue promptly.
>
> **Example 14:** Sorry, not my prob. deal with it.
>
> **Example 15:** A contract with well-defined terms and conditions, written in plain language.
>
> **Example 16:** A contract with convoluted language and ambiguous clauses.

Class Activity 3: *Poor writing will lead to misunderstandings and missed opportunities in various professional contexts. Point out the problems in the following sentences, including grammatical errors.*

1. Please revise the report and make it better.

2. E-mail Subject Line: Important

3. Their launching a new product they're.

4. Proposal: We have a great idea for a partnership. Let us know if interested.

5. While walking to the office, the car broke down.

6. John told Sarah that he will be late.

7. Reports: Sales are down by 20%.

8. Contracts: A contract's missing details like payment terms, project milestones, and dispute resolution mechanisms.

Class Activity 4: *Try to fill in the blanks of a student's self-reflection worksheet.*

Name: _____   Date: _____

Instructions: Take some time to reflect on your current writing skills and challenges. Be honest in your responses as this will help you identify areas for improvement.

Part 1: Self-Assessment

1. Rate Your Confidence

On a scale of 1 to 5, rate your confidence in your overall writing skills (1—Not confident at all, 5—Very confident).

Overall Writing Skills: Grammar and Punctuation:

Vocabulary and Word Choice: Clarity and Organization:

2. Identify Your Strengths

(List two areas where you feel confident and proficient in your writing.)

_____

_____

_____

_____

3. Recognize Your Challenges

(List two areas where you feel you need improvement in your writing.)

_____

_____

_____

_____

Part 2: Reflective Questions

1. What Types of Writing Have You Done?

(List any types of writing you have encountered, such as essays, e-mails, reports, etc.)

_____

_____

_____

_____

2. What Aspects of Writing Do You Enjoy?
(Describe what aspects of writing you find enjoyable or engaging.)

_____

_____

_____

3. What Aspects of Writing Do You Find Challenging?
(Explain which aspects of writing you struggle with or find difficult.)

_____

_____

_____

4. How Do You Typically Approach the Writing Process?
(Describe your usual approach when you start writing, including any planning or brainstorming methods.)

_____

_____

_____

5. Are There Specific Grammar or Punctuation Rules You Struggle with?
(Share any particular grammar or punctuation rules that you find confusing or challenging.)

_____

_____

_____

Part 3: Goal Setting

1. What Do You Hope to Achieve in This Course?
(Outline your goals for improving your writing skills during this course.)

_____

_____

_____

2. How Will You Address Your Writing Challenges?
(Describe the steps you plan to take to overcome the challenges you have identified.)

_____

_____

_____

3. Additional Comments or Questions

(Feel free to provide any additional comments, questions, or concerns you may have about improving your writing skills.)

_____

_____

_____

Part 4: Conclusion

Reflecting on your current skills and challenges is the first step towards becoming a better writer. Use this worksheet as a guide to identify areas for growth and set goals for improvement. Your commitment to enhancing your writing skills will contribute to your success in this course and beyond.

Signature: _____

Unit 2
Writing Basics

Unit 2 delves into the foundational elements of effective writing, emphasizing the importance of understanding and mastering writing basics. Through a structured exploration of the writing process, the purpose behind writing, the choice of tone and style, and audience awareness, this unit offers a comprehensive framework for students looking to enhance their writing skills.

2.1
Understanding the Writing Process

Effective writing is a skill that involves a systematic process to convey ideas, information, or messages clearly and persuasively. This section explores the writing process and its key stages, empowering you to approach any writing task with confidence and a well-organized structure.

2.1.1 Prewriting

Prewriting is the initial stage where you brainstorm ideas, gather information, and plan your approach. Consider your purpose, audience, and the message you want to convey. Create outlines, mind maps, or notes to organize your thoughts and identify key points.

Class Activity 1: *Read the following examples of prewriting practice in real-life business communication and discuss your understanding with your classmates.*

Example 1: Writing a Business E-mail

Lucy needs to write an e-mail to her team about a new project's kickoff

---

meeting. Here's how she goes through the prewriting stages:

- **Brainstorm Ideas:** Think about the main points she wants to cover in the e-mail. Consider the agenda, meeting date, time, and location.
- **Gather Information:** Collect all the relevant details about the project's kickoff meeting, such as the project name, objectives, and any necessary attachments.
- **Identify Purpose and Audience:** Define the purpose of the e-mail—to inform her team about the upcoming meeting. Consider her audience—her team members—and what information they need to know.
- **Plan Approach:** Decide on the tone of the e-mail—professional and informative. Determine the key sections of the e-mail, including the introduction, meeting details, and a call to action.
- **Create Outline or Notes:** Write a brief outline that includes bullet points for each section of the e-mail. This helps her organize her thoughts and ensures that she covers all the essential information.

Example 2: Writing a Business Report

Now, let's consider the prewriting process for writing a quarterly sales report:

- **Brainstorm Ideas:** Reflect on the sales data you have and the trends you've observed over the past quarter. Consider the key metrics you want to highlight.
- **Gather Information:** Collect the sales data, revenue figures, customer feedback, and any other relevant information that will contribute to your report.
- **Identify Purpose and Audience:** Define the purpose of the report—to analyze sales performance and provide insights. Consider your audience—your colleagues and supervisors—who will use the report to make informed decisions.
- **Plan Approach:** Decide on the structure of the report, including sections like Executive Summary, Sales Performance Analysis, Key Takeaways, and Recommendations.
- **Create Outline or Mind Map:** Create a visual mind map that outlines the main sections of the report and the subtopics you'll cover within each section. This visual representation helps you see the big picture.

In both examples, the prewriting process involves brainstorming, gathering information, defining purpose and audience, planning the approach, and creating an outline or visual aid. This stage lays the foundation for the rest of the writing process, ensuring that your content is well-organized, focused, and aligned with your goals.

Class Activity 2: *Read the following examples of prewriting techniques and discuss the prewriting techniques and experiences with your classmates.*

1. Brainstorming

Topic: Improving Employee Engagement in the Workplace

Individual Brainstorming: Students can individually jot down any ideas, keywords, or concepts related to the topic. For example:

- Recognition programs;
- Employee feedback surveys;
- Team-building activities;
- Flexible work arrangements;
- Professional development opportunities.

Group Brainstorming: In pairs or groups, students can verbally share their ideas related to the topic. The facilitator can note down these ideas on a whiteboard or flip chart. This encourages the generation of collaborative ideas.

2. Mind Mapping

Topic: Marketing Strategies for a New Product Launch

Students can create a mind map using a central topic or keyword (e.g., New Product Launch) and branch out with related ideas. For example:

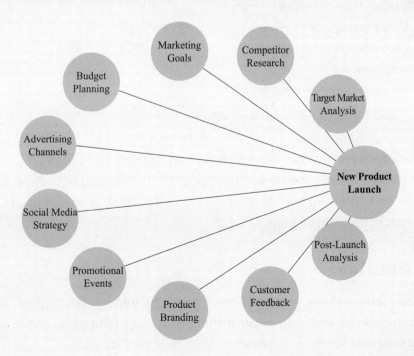

3. Outlining

Topic: Proposal for a Team-Building Workshop

Students can create a structured outline that helps organize their ideas logically before writing the actual content. For example:

Introduction:

- Hook to grab attention;
- Brief overview of the workshop's purpose;
- Importance of team building.

Workshop Content:

- Ice-breaking activities;
- Communication exercises;
- Problem-solving challenges;
- Leadership development sessions.

Benefits of the Workshop:

- Enhancing team cohesion;
- Improving communication skills;
- Boosting morale and productivity.

Logistics and Budget:

- Duration and schedule;
- Venue and resources required;
- Estimated budget breakdown.

Conclusion:

- Recap of workshop's value;
- Call to action for further discussion.

Each of these prewriting activities serves as a valuable starting point for students to gather ideas, structure their thoughts, and plan their writing effectively. They can choose the prewriting method that best suits their thinking style and the specific requirements of their writing task.

2.1.2 Drafting

At the drafting stage, you transform your ideas into written content. Focus on getting your thoughts down on paper without worrying about perfection. Allow your creativity to flow, and aim to capture the essence of your message.

2.1.3 Revising

Revision is the process of reviewing and refining your draft for clarity, coherence, and effectiveness. Consider the organization of your content, the flow of ideas, and the strength of your arguments. Make necessary changes to improve the overall quality of your writing.

2.1.4 Editing

Editing involves checking for grammar, spelling, punctuation, and style errors. Pay attention to sentence structure, word choice, and consistency. Edit your work with precision to ensure your writing is polished and error-free.

2.1.5 Proofreading

Proofreading is the final step before sharing your work. It involves carefully reviewing your document to catch any remaining errors or inconsistencies. Read your writing aloud or ask someone else to review it for a fresh perspective.

Remember, the writing process is not always linear—you may find yourself revisiting earlier stages as you refine your work. Embrace each step, and with practice, you'll develop a writing process that suits your style and produces impactful results.

By understanding and embracing the writing process, you'll gain the tools you need to produce the well-crafted, effective written communication in any professional context. As you progress through this textbook, keep these foundational principles in mind to enhance your business English writing skills.

Class Activity 3: *Work in pairs to identify and correct the errors in the following e-mail.*

Subject: Meeting Reminder and Preparations

Hi team,

Just wanted to remind everyone about the meeting next week. It will be held on Tuesday at 2:30 p. m. The purpose of the meeting is to discuss the upcoming project, and the manager will give their presentation. Please be prepared for the discussion. Also, don't forget to bring you're notes and ideas.

Thanks,

John

2.2
Understanding the Writing Purpose

Effective business English writing is rooted in a clear understanding of your writing purpose. The purpose guides your content, tone, and structure, ensuring that your message resonates with your audience and achieves your intended goals. This section delves into the importance of understanding the writing purpose and how to align your approach accordingly.

2.2.1 Common Purposes for Business Writing

To Inform: Business writing may be used to provide information for colleagues, clients, or stakeholders. This could include things like reports, updates, or memos.

To Persuade: Business writing may also be used to persuade others to take a specific action or adopt a particular point of view. This could include things like proposals, sales letters, or marketing copy.

To Instruct: Business writing may also be used to provide instructions or guidelines. This could include things like training materials, user manuals, or standard operating procedures.

Class Activity 4: *Identify the purpose of each scenario and provide your justification.*

Example: Writing an E-mail to a Client
Primary Purpose: <u>Persuading</u>
Justification: <u>The e-mail aims to convince the client to consider a new product or service. The language might highlight benefits and value propositions.</u>
Scenario 1: Drafting a Proposal for a Business Partnership
Primary Purpose: _____
Justification: _____
Scenario 2: Sending a Memo to Colleagues About New Office Policies
Primary Purpose: _____
Justification: _____
Scenario 3: Composing an E-mail Requesting Additional Budget Allocation
Primary Purpose: _____

Justification: _____

Scenario 4: Writing a Thank-You E-mail to a Vendor After Successful Collaboration

Primary Purpose: _____

Justification: _____

Scenario 5: Crafting an Internal Newsletter to Share Company Updates

Primary Purpose: _____

Justification: _____

Scenario 6: Preparing a Sales Pitch Presentation for Potential Investors

Primary Purpose: _____

Justification: _____

Scenario 7: Writing a Condolence E-mail to an Employee Who Lost a Family Member

Primary Purpose: _____

Justification: _____

2.2.2 The Audience for Business Writing

Customers/Clients: Individuals or organizations that purchase your products or services. Their satisfaction is vital for maintaining business relationships and securing future transactions.

Colleagues/Peers: Your co-workers and colleagues within your organization. Effective communication among team members ensures smooth workflow and successful project outcomes.

Supervisors/Managers: Your immediate superiors that provide guidance, assign tasks, and evaluate your performance. Clear communication with managers helps set expectations and showcase your accomplishments.

Shareholders/Investors: Individuals or entities that invested financially in the company. Your communication can impact their perception of the company's direction and performance.

Suppliers/Partners: Businesses that provide resources, materials, or services for your organization. Open communication with suppliers ensures the timely delivery of necessary components.

Government/Regulatory Bodies: Organizations that oversee compliance with laws and regulations. Accurate communication is crucial to meet legal obligations.

Media/Public: Journalists, media outlets, and the general public that may require information about your company. Maintaining a positive public image through effective communication is essential.

2.2.3 Audience and Purpose Combinations

The purpose of business English writing is to communicate effectively in a professional setting. The audience for business writing can vary widely, depending on the specific context and purpose of the communication. For example:

> Purpose: To inform; Audience: Colleagues.
>
> Purpose: To persuade; Audience: Clients.
>
> Purpose: To instruct; Audience: Regulators.

In all cases, it's important for the writer to understand his or her purpose and the audience to ensure that the writing is effective and achieves its intended goals.

2.2.4 Aligning Your Approach

Understanding your writing purpose allows you to align your approach to the specific needs of your readers. Consider the following scenarios:

Informative Writing: If your purpose is to inform, focus on presenting clear and accurate information. The tone should be objective, and you should provide the necessary details without bias. For example:

> **The Importance of Bees in Pollination**
>
> Bees play a crucial role in the pollination of many crops and wild plants, ensuring the production of fruit, seeds, and more. As pollinators, bees transfer pollen from the male parts of a flower to the female parts, facilitating the plant's ability to grow seeds and reproduce. This process is vital for the health of ecosystems and for agricultural production, as approximately one-third of the food we consume each day relies on pollination primarily by bees. Understanding their role highlights the importance of protecting bee populations and their habitats.

Persuasive Writing: When persuading, your purpose is to convince your audience to take a specific action or adopt your viewpoint. Use compelling arguments, evidence, and a persuasive tone to influence their decisions. For example:

The Benefits of Solar Energy

Solar energy stands out as the most viable and sustainable solution to our growing energy needs. By harnessing the power of the Sun, we can reduce our dependence on fossil fuels, decrease pollution, and combat climate change. Solar panels provide a clean, renewable source of energy that can significantly lower electricity bills. Moreover, advancements in technology have made solar systems more efficient and affordable than ever. I urge you to consider the long-term environmental and economic benefits of solar energy and to invest in solar panels for your home or business today.

Instructional Writing: In instructional writing, guide your readers through a process, step by step. Use clear instructions and consider their background knowledge to ensure clarity. For example:

How to Make French Press Coffee

To make French press coffee, you'll need coarse ground coffee, boiling water, and a French press. Begin by adding one tablespoon of coffee per four ounces of water into the press. Pour hot water—not quite boiling—over the grounds, ensuring all the coffee is submerged. Stir the mixture gently, and then place the lid on the press with the plunger pulled all the way up. Let the coffee steep for four minutes. Slowly press the plunger down, separating the grounds from the liquid. Serve the coffee immediately to enjoy its full flavor. Remember, the quality of the coffee beans and the ratio of coffee to water can be adjusted to taste.

Entertaining Writing: In entertaining writing, engage your readers with anecdotes, humor, or relatable content. Your tone can be more relaxed, reflecting the desired mood. For example:

The Adventures of a Weekend Hiker

Last weekend's hiking trip was supposed to be relaxing, yet there I was, dangling from a branch, questioning my life choices. It all started with what I believed was a shortcut. Spoiler alert: It wasn't. As I ventured off the beaten path, the sounds of civilization faded, replaced by the rustling of leaves and my increasingly loud complaints. The shortcut led me to a muddy slope, which I descended with all the grace of a newborn giraffe. There, amidst the mud and laughter from my friends, I found a new appreciation for the well-trodden path. It's safe to say that my hiking escapades provided more entertainment than intended, especially for those watching my mud-splattered return to the trailhead.

2.2.5 Tailoring for the Audience

Understanding your audience is equally important. Tailor your content to their needs, preferences, and expectations. A professional report for colleagues will differ from a social media post targeting potential customers. Consider their familiarity with the topic, their concerns, and the level of formality they expect. For example:

Informative Writing

Professional Report for Colleagues

Topic: Annual Market Trends Report

This comprehensive report examines the fluctuating trends in the global markets with a focus on the impacts of recent economic policies. Our analysis reveals key patterns that could influence our strategic investments and business decisions. Detailed charts and statistics are included to provide a thorough understanding of market dynamics.

Social Media Post for General Public

Topic: Quick Facts About Recycling

Did you know that recycling a single aluminum can save enough energy to run a TV for three hours? Let's make a difference together! Start recycling today and help us save our planet, one can at a time. #RecycleMore #EcoFriendly

Persuasive Writing

Proposal to Management

Topic: Implementing Remote Working Policy

E-mail Campaign to Customers

Topic: Promotion of a New Eco-friendly Product

As we adapt to the changing business landscape, introducing a remote working policy can significantly enhance employee productivity and satisfaction. Our analysis indicates a potential increase in productivity by 20% and reduced operational costs. The following proposal outlines the benefits and strategies for effective implementation.

Are you ready to be a part of the green revolution? Our latest eco-friendly product is not just good for the environment; it's great for you too! With a special 20% discount for our loyal customers, there's never been a better time to go green. Shop now and join us in making a difference!

Instructional Writing

Technical Manual for Engineers

Topic: Installation of Industrial Machinery

Section 4.2: Calibration Procedure. Ensure the machinery is in manual mode before beginning calibration. Use the XYZ gauge for precision alignment, referring to Diagram 17-B for the specific measurements. Note: Calibration must be performed in a temperature-controlled environment to maintain accuracy.

Blog Post for Hobbyists

Topic: Basic Gardening Tips for Beginners

Hey green thumbs! New to gardening? Start with something simple like succulents or herbs. Remember, plants need good soil, a bit of sunshine, and a lot of love. Water them when the soil feels dry but don't overdo it. Happy gardening!

Entertaining Writing

Novel for Young Adults

Topic: A Magical Summer Adventure

That summer in Ravenwood was unlike any other. Ellie discovered a hidden world of magic, with talking

Post for a Parenting Blog

Topic: The Joys and Chaos of Parenting Toddlers

Parenting toddlers is like being on a rollercoaster that never stops. One

> animals and enchanted forests. With her newfound friends, she embarked on a quest that would not only test their courage but reveal secrets that would change their lives forever.
>
> minute, you're laughing as they dance in a rain puddle; the next, you're chasing a mini escape artist covered in marker art. Embrace the chaos, cherish the cuddles, and remember, coffee is your best friend.

In each example, the content is tailored to suit the specific audience's preferences, background knowledge, and the level of formality expected, demonstrating a clear understanding of the target audience.

Understanding the purpose of your writing is like setting the course for a journey. It ensures that your message reaches its destination effectively and leaves a lasting impact. By recognizing your purpose and adapting your approach accordingly, you'll craft communication that engages, informs, and influences your specific audience with precision.

2.3
Choosing the Right Tone and Style

The tone and style you employ in your business English writing play a pivotal role in conveying your message effectively and establishing the desired impression. This section explores the nuances of choosing the appropriate tone and style, allowing you to adapt your communication to different contexts and audiences.

Tone refers to the attitude or emotion that your writing conveys. It influences how your message is perceived—whether it's formal, casual, authoritative, friendly, or empathetic. Style pertains to how you express your ideas. It encompasses sentence structure, word choice, and overall language use.

Adapting your tone and style requires considering both your audience and your purpose. Here's how to strike the right balance.

2.3.1 Formality vs. Informality

You should choose the level of formality based on the context of your writing. Formality suits official documents, reports, and professional correspondence, while informality is suitable for internal communication, e-mails to colleagues, or social media updates.

Class Activity 5: *Read the two e-mails to identify and highlight the elements that make one e-mail formal and the other informal.*

Formal:

Dear Mr. Johnson,

I am writing to inquire about the availability of your consulting services for our upcoming project. We have reviewed your impressive portfolio and believe your expertise aligns well with our needs. Could you please provide us with more information about your availability and pricing?

Thank you for your prompt attention.

Sincerely,

Mike Brown

Informal:

Hey Jack,

Hope you're doing well! Wanted to chat about possibly teaming up for our next project. Your work is amazing and seems like a great fit. Could you shoot me some info on availability and what it might cost?

Catch you later,

Mike

Class Activity 6: *Share examples of how inappropriate tone and style can lead to misunderstandings or misinterpretations.*

Example: Overly Formal Tone in Team E-mail:

Subject: Team Event Coordination Meeting

Dear Team,

I hereby request your presence at an upcoming coordination meeting to discuss the logistics and planning of our casual team-building event. Your prompt attendance is expected, and please prepare a detailed report on your respective responsibilities.

Regards,

Mark

Result: Using an overly formal tone for a casual team event can make team members feel uncomfortable and reluctant to participate.

Class Activity 7: *Identify and align each tone on the left with the intended purpose on the right.*

1. Writing an e-mail to a client to introduce a new product

2. Preparing a presentation for a board meeting

3. Drafting a thank-you e-mail to a colleague for his or her help on a project

4. Responding to a formal complaint from a customer

5. Writing a memo to inform employees about a change in company policies

6. Composing a press release to announce a new partnership

a. Promoting
   Professional and upbeat

b. Persuading
   Informal and enthusiastic

c. Informing
   Formal and directive

d. Resolving
   Polite and empathetic

e. Informing
   Formal and factual

f. Expressing gratitude
   Friendly and appreciative

Class Activity 8: *Write an e-mail to a classmate requesting his or her assistance with a task.*

2.3.2 Clarity and Simplicity

You should prioritize clarity by using clear and concise sentences. Avoid jargon and overly complex language that might confuse your audience. For example:

- **Clear and Concise:** Our quarterly earnings have increased by 15% compared with the previous year.
- **Jargon:** Our QoQ earnings have surged by 15% YoY.
- **Clear and Concise:** We need your decision by Friday to proceed with the project.
- **Overly Complex:** Your prompt resolution to this matter is requisite by close of business on Friday in order to facilitate the advancement of the project.
- **Clear and Concise:** Please find the attached report you requested.
- **Jargon:** Enclosed herewith, please locate the report as per your earlier request.

- **Clear and Concise:** We'll meet at 3 p.m. to discuss the budget.
- **Overly Complex:** A gathering is scheduled for 3 p.m. for the purpose of conducting a discussion pertaining to the budget.

Using jargon or overly complex language can make communication unclear and alienate the audience. Striving for simplicity and clarity to ensure your message is easily understood by a broader range of readers. Avoiding unnecessary technical terms and convoluted sentences helps you create more effective and accessible business communication.

2.3.3 Audience Engagement

You should tailor your tone and style to resonate with your audience's preferences. Engaging with them on a relatable level without sacrificing professionalism is important. For example:

- We are pleased to announce our latest product line, which boasts cutting-edge features and unparalleled functionality. This product is destined to revolutionize the industry and set new benchmarks for performance.
- Exciting news! Our brand-new product line is here, packed with amazing features that will transform how you work. We can't wait to show you how it's going to make your life easier and more productive.

In the first example, the language is formal and contains jargon that might not resonate with a broader audience. Although it sounds professional, it might not engage readers who aren't familiar with technical terms.

The second example adopts a more relatable and enthusiastic tone. It uses simpler language, employs positive adjectives, and focuses on how the product benefits the audience. This approach is more likely to captivate the reader's attention and create a connection, leading to better engagement.

Remember, engaging with your audience effectively requires understanding their preferences, needs, and communication styles. Tailoring your tone and style accordingly can significantly enhance the impact of your business communication.

2.3.4 Purpose-Driven Approach

You should align your tone and style with your purpose. If you're persuading, adopt a persuasive tone and use compelling language. If you're informing, opt for an objective and informative style. For example:

Persuasive Communication:

- Objective: We would appreciate your consideration of our proposal.
  Purpose-driven: We believe that our innovative solution can significantly enhance your operational efficiency. Join us in this transformative journey.
- Objective: Please attend the event.
  Purpose-driven: Don't miss out on this exclusive event. Your presence will contribute to its success and make it an unforgettable experience.

Informative Communication:

- Objective: The meeting will take place on Friday at 2 p.m.
- Purpose-driven: Mark your calendars! Our next meeting is scheduled for this Friday at 2 p.m. Here's the agenda.
- Objective: The report is ready for review.
- Purpose-driven: Great news! The report you've been waiting for is now ready for your review. It provides insights that can shape our next steps.

In the purpose-driven approach, the tone and style of communication are tailored to achieve a specific goal. When persuading, the language is compelling and encourages action. When informing, the focus is on providing clear and objective information. Aligning your tone and style with your purpose ensures that your message resonates effectively with your audience and achieves the desired outcome.

Unit 3
Business Writing Skills

Unit 3 focuses on refining business writing skills, which are essential for effective and impactful communication in any professional setting. This unit covers key areas from spotlighting reader benefits and expressing positively to using inclusive language and balancing conversational tone with professionalism.

Section 3.1 explores how to shift from writer-oriented to reader-oriented messages, emphasizing the benefits to the audience to foster positive connections. Section 3.2 delves into the power of positive language, focusing on how to frame messages that encourage solutions and constructive action. Section 3.3 is dedicated to inclusive language, guiding you to write in ways that respect and acknowledge diversity, and avoid bias. Section 3.4 balances conversational and professional language, offering tips to keep your writing engaging yet respectful. Sections 3.5 and 3.6 introduce emphatic and de-emphatic devices, showing how to highlight or soften the impact of your message.

By the end of this unit, you'll master the art of crafting clear, respectful, and impactful business communication that resonates with a diverse audience.

3.1
Spotlighting the Reader's Benefits

When crafting effective business communication, focusing on the reader's perspective is paramount. This approach, often referred to as adopting the "you" view, fundamentally shifts the focus from the writer's intent to the reader's benefits. By spotlighting the reader's benefits, the message becomes more engaging, persuasive, and impactful. This section delves into the importance of emphasizing reader benefits, which can make business writing more reader-oriented and effective.

3.1.1 From Writer-Oriented to Reader-Oriented

Switching from a writer-oriented to a reader-oriented perspective involves reframing statements to highlight how the reader stands to gain or benefit. This technique not only makes your message more compelling but also enhances your readers' engagement by directly addressing their interests and needs. For example:

- **Writer-Oriented:** To enable us to update our stockholder records, we ask that the enclosed card should be returned.
- **Reader-Oriented:** To make sure that you may promptly receive dividend checks and information related to your shares, please return the enclosed card.

The reader-oriented version directly conveys the benefits to the readers, making the action of returning the enclosed card more appealing.

3.1.2 Enhancing Response and Action

Clear communication about the benefits encourages the readers to respond or take action positively. This approach is particularly effective when the goal is to prompt immediate action or participation. For example:

- **Writer-Oriented:** The Human Resources Department requires that the enclosed questionnaire be completed immediately so that we can allocate our training resource funds.
- **Reader-Oriented:** By filling out the enclosed questionnaire, you can be one of the first employees to sign up for the new career development program.

This reframing positions the action not as a requirement but as an opportunity for the readers, enhancing their motivation to comply.

3.1.3 Adopting the "You" View in Marketing

In marketing, the "you" view is instrumental in crafting messages that resonate with potential customers, emphasizing how products or services fit into their lives. For example:

> • **Writer-Oriented:** We offer an online business writing course that we have complete faith in.
> • **Reader-Oriented:** Improve your business writing skills and sign up for our online course! The sooner you sign up, the sooner the rewards will be yours.

Such a shift not only highlights the direct benefits to the readers but also creates a sense of urgency and personal investment.

3.1.4 Avoiding Negative Connotations

While the "you" view is powerful, it's important to use it judiciously, especially in contexts where it might convey a negative message or impose an unwelcome requirement. For example:

> • **Negative Context:** You cannot return merchandise until you receive the written approval.
> • **Positive Reframing:** Customers may return merchandise with the written approval.

This approach maintains a focus on the policy while avoiding direct negative implications for the readers.

Spotlighting reader benefits by adopting the "you" view transforms business writing from merely informative to engaging and persuasive. This method of organization emphasizes the reader's interests, encourages positive action, and fosters a more personal connection between the message and its audience. Whether drafting business documents, crafting marketing materials, or communicating policies, focusing on how the content benefits the reader can significantly enhance the effectiveness of your communication.

Class Activity 1: *Rewrite the following sentences to spotlight the reader's benefits.*
1. Our software features advanced encryption technology.
2. Our vacuum cleaners have a battery life of up to 60 minutes.

3. The new app includes a feature for tracking your daily water intake.

Class Activity 2: *Rewrite the following sentences to employ the "you" view, making them more reader-oriented and focused on the reader's benefits.*

1. The company has extended its customer service hours.

2. We offer a 20% discount on all first-time orders through our website.

3. Our team provides personalized investment advice tailored to individual financial goals.

4. The latest software update includes enhanced security features for user protection.

Class Activity 3: *Create two ad slogans that highlight the convenience and benefits to the customer.*

3.2
Expressing Positively

In the realm of business writing, the power of positive expressions cannot be overstated. Adopting a positive tone not only reflects a proactive and solution-oriented approach but also significantly impacts the reader's perception and response. This section explores the concept of positive expressions, illustrating how rephrasing statements with a positive spin can transform communication, enhance relationships, and foster a constructive environment.

3.2.1 The Shift to Positive Language

Positive expressions focus on what can be done rather than what cannot. They are about framing messages in a way that highlights possibilities, solutions, and positive outcomes. This approach encourages a more receptive and collaborative response from the audience. For example:

- **Negative:** Employees may not use the First Street entrance during remodeling.
- **Positive:** Employees may use the Market Street entrance during remodeling.

3.2.2 Emphasizing Solutions over Problems

By emphasizing solutions, you can direct attention to positive actions and outcomes, which can motivate and inspire the intended audience. This strategy is particularly effective in addressing challenges, offering feedback, or communicating requirements. For example:

- **Negative:** We cannot fill your order until we receive an exact model number.
- **Positive:** We can fill your order once we receive an exact model number.

3.2.3 Learning from Negative Outcomes

Even when outcomes are not as expected, expressing the situation positively can turn a setback into a learning opportunity. This fosters a culture of continuous improvement and resilience. For example:

- **Negative:** We wasted $300,000 advertising in that magazine.
- **Positive:** Our $300,000 advertising investment did not pay off. Let's analyze the experience and apply the insights to future campaigns.

3.2.4 Reframing Feedback

Positive reframing is crucial for providing feedback or addressing issues. It can prevent defensiveness and encourage a constructive dialog. For example:

- **Negative:** The problem would not have happened if you had connected the wires properly.
- **Positive:** The problem may be resolved by connecting the wires as shown in the handbook.

3.2.5 Encouraging Action

Encouraging specific action through positive phrasing can guide behavior in a desirable direction without resorting to threats or negative consequences. For example:

- **Negative:** We will notify all three credit reporting agencies if you do not pay your overdue bill within 10 days.
- **Positive:** Paying your overdue bill within 10 days will prevent a negative entry on your credit record.

3.2.6 Avoiding Negative Expressions

Certain expressions inherently carry a negative connotation and can hinder effective communication. Replacing them with positive or neutral terms can alter the tone of the message significantly. For example:

- **Negative:** You failed to deliver the customer's order on time.
- **Positive:** Let's figure out a system that will ensure on-time deliveries.

3.2.7 The Role of Positive Words

Choosing positive words with emotional associations can subtly influence the reader's feelings and reactions, enhancing the overall impact of the message. For example:

- **Negative:** Jeff is hung up on trivial details.
- **Positive:** Jeff is meticulous; he takes care of details that others often ignore.

Expressing positively is a strategic choice in business communication that can lead to more effective interactions, foster goodwill, and promote a productive and constructive organizational culture. By focusing on solutions, possibilities, and positive outcomes, writers and speakers can inspire action, facilitate understanding, and build stronger relationships with their audience.

Class Activity 4: *Reframe the negatives to positives to focus on the reader's benefits with a positive tone and without directly using "you" in a negative context.*

1. We don't offer support on weekends.
2. Failure to comply with these regulations will result in penalties.

3. You must not use company devices for personal browsing.

4. We cannot process your application without the mandatory documents.

5. You must wait 24 hours before your account is activated.

6. We don't offer refunds after 30 days from purchase.

Class Activity 5: *Convert the following negative feedback into constructive proposals that spotlight benefits to the readers.*

1. You failed to deliver the customer's order on time.

2. The report contained several inaccuracies.

3. The client presentation didn't address all the project requirements.

4. Team meetings do not result in actionable decisions.

5. Customer support responses are taking too long.

Class Activity 6: *Transform the following sentences into positive statements focusing on professional use benefits.*

1. You must not use company phones for personal calls.

2. Employees are not allowed to take office supplies home.

3. Don't submit reports without proofreading them first.

4. You must not ignore e-mails from clients.

5. Employees should not leave their workstations unclean.

3.3
Inclusive Language

The adoption of inclusive language in business writing is not only a matter of political correctness but also a fundamental aspect of effective communication that respects and acknowledges diversity. Inclusive language seeks to avoid bias, be it gender, age, disability, race, ethnicity, or LGBT (lesbian, gay, bisexual and transgender) communities, ensuring that communication is universally respectful and welcoming to all.

3.3.1 Overcoming Gender Bias

Gender bias in language can inadvertently alienate or make assumptions about the readers. The following example shows some ways to address and neutralize gender bias:

- **Gender-Biased:** Every homeowner must read his insurance policy carefully.
- **Inclusive Alternatives:**
  ☐ All homeowners must read their insurance policy carefully. (use a plural noun and pronoun)
  ☐ Every homeowner must read the insurance policy carefully. (omit the pronoun entirely)
  ☐ Every homeowner must read his or her insurance policy carefully. (use both masculine and feminine pronouns)

3.3.2 Neutralizing Job Titles

Many traditional job titles carry gender bias that can be easily rectified with neutral alternatives. For example:

Gender-Biased		Inclusive
salesman	→	salesperson or sales representative
fireman	→	firefighter
chairman	→	chair
policeman	→	police officer

3.3.3 Addressing Age Bias

Language can also inadvertently express bias towards individuals based on age, which can be corrected by focusing on the action or role rather than the age. For example:

- **Age-Biased:** The law applies to old people.
- **Inclusive:** The law applies to people over 65.

3.3.4 Eliminating Racial and Ethnic Bias

Avoid mentioning any race or ethnicity unless it is relevant to the context, ensuring that individuals are recognized first and foremost for their actions or roles. For example:

- **Biased:** An Indian accountant was hired.
- **Inclusive:** An accountant was hired.

3.3.5 Disability Awareness

Language surrounding disabilities should focus on the person first, rather than the disability, to emphasize ability over limitation. For example:

- **Biased:** Handicapped employees face many barriers on the job.
- **Inclusive:** Workers with physical disabilities face many barriers on the job.

3.3.6 Using Inclusive Terms for Humanity

Even broader terms that have traditionally been used can be updated for inclusivity. For example, "mankind" is a gender-biased word and "humanity" or "human race" is a better choice.

Using inclusive language in business writing fosters an environment of respect, equality, and diversity. It reflects a conscious effort to recognize and value the wide range of human experiences and identities. By being mindful of your word choices, you can make your communication more welcoming and inclusive to all, thereby enriching your professional interactions and relationships.

Class Activity 7: *Rewrite the following biased statements to make them more inclusive.*

1. The new engineer must submit his report by next Monday.
2. A successful businessman knows how to delegate tasks.
3. Each stewardess is responsible for passenger safety during flights.
4. Man-made materials are often cheaper than natural ones.
5. The chairman will address the shareholders at the annual meeting.

3.4
Conversational but Professional Language

In the realm of business writing, striking a perfect balance between being conversational and professional is essential for effective communication. This approach ensures the message is accessible and engaging while maintaining the respect and formality expected in professional settings. This section will explore strategies to achieve this balance, enhancing the clarity and impact of business communication.

3.4.1 The Spectrum of Business Writing

Business writing often falls into three categories: too formal, too informal, or conversational yet professional. Understanding and navigating this spectrum is crucial for crafting messages that resonate with the audience without compromising professionalism.

- **Too formal writing** tends to use big words, technical jargon, or old-fashioned expressions that may create distance or obscure the meaning of the message.

- **Too informal writing** relies on slang, acronyms, or overly casual language that can undermine seriousness or professionalism of the message.

- **Conversational but professional writing** strikes a balance between a clear, straightforward language and a polite, respectful tone. This approach makes the message accessible without being overly casual.

3.4.2 Avoiding Extremes

To maintain a conversational but professional tone, it's important to avoid the extremes of being too casual or too formal. This involves understanding the difference between texting and professional writing, avoiding slang and acronyms, and using humor and intimacy with caution. For example:

- **Too Casual:** Plz be informed that u are nominated 2 attend the Risk Management seminar @ Hilton Hotel.

- **Too Formal:** Enclosed, please find the information requested during our telephone communication.
- **Conversational but Professional:** Here's the information you requested. Our seminar on Risk Management will be held at the Hilton Hotel.

3.4.3 Using Modern Expressions

Replacing old-fashioned expressions with modern, straightforward language can make the message more relatable and easier to understand. For example:

- **Old-Fashioned:** As per your request, enclosed herewith please find...
- **Modern and Conversational:** At your request, I've attached...

3.4.4 Avoiding Technical Jargon and Big Words

Use technical jargon judiciously, ensuring it's appropriate for the audience's knowledge level. Avoid unnecessary big words that might alienate or confuse the audience. For example:

- **Technical and Inaccessible:** Our offerings include leading-edge service configuration assurance capabilities.
- **Conversational and Accessible:** We offer advanced services to ensure your setup is reliable and meets your needs.

3.4.5 Choosing the Right Levels of Diction

Choosing the right level of diction is key to remaining professional without being overly formal or casual. For example:

- **Unprofessional:** If we hang in there, we can snag the contract.
- **Formal:** If the principals persevere, they can secure the contract.
- **Conversational but Professional:** If we stay focused, we can win the contract.

3.4.6 Practical Tips for Conversational Professionalism

1. **Being Clear and Direct**

   Use simple, direct language that conveys your message without ambiguity.

   The following examples demonstrate the shift from the ambiguous or overly complex language to simple and direct expressions.

Less Clear and Direct	Clearer and More Direct
Example 1: Providing Instructions	
"It is requested that the submission of the documents be expedited by the concerned parties at their earliest convenience."	"Please submit the documents as soon as possible."
Example 2: Making a Request	
"Would it be too much of an imposition to ask for your assistance in the matter concerning the upcoming project?"	"Can you help with the upcoming project?"
Example 3: Offering Assistance	
"Should you find yourself in a situation where assistance is deemed necessary, do not hesitate to make your requirements known to me."	"If you need help, please let me know."
Example 4: Scheduling a Meeting	
"In the interest of facilitating a collaborative discussion regarding the matters at hand, it would be advantageous to arrange for a congregation of the involved parties at a mutually agreeable juncture."	"Let's schedule a meeting to discuss this."
Example 5: Feedback on Work	
"There are certain aspects of your recent submis-sion that might benefit from a further detailed examination and subsequent enhancement to align more closely with the original specifications outlined."	"Your recent work needs some revisions to meet the project's requirements."

These examples show that using simple, direct language can make communication more effective, reducing the likelihood of misunderstanding and increasing the efficiency of interaction.

2. Maintaining Respect

Always show respect for the readers, regardless of the informality of the language.

The following examples demonstrate how to keep language respectful, even when adopting a more informal or conversational tone.

Less Respectful	More Respectful
Example 1: Addressing a Concern "I don't see why you're making such a big deal out of this."	"I understand your concerns and take them seriously. Let's work together to find a solution."
Example 2: Denying a Request "No, we can't do that. It's against our policy."	"I understand your request, but unfortunately, it's not something we can accommodate due to our current policy. I'm here to explore other options with you."
Example 3: Providing Feedback "This report is poorly done. Did you even review it before submitting?"	"Thank you for submitting the report. I believe it could benefit from further review for more detailed insights."
Example 4: Requesting Information You haven't sent the information I asked for. You need to send it now.	"Could you please send the information I requested at your earliest convenience? Thank you."
Example 5: Addressing a Missed Deadline "You missed the deadline again. What's your excuse this time?"	"I noticed the deadline was missed. Can we discuss how to prevent this in the future?"

These examples demonstrate that maintaining a tone of respect is possible even in informal or direct communication. By showing understanding, appreciation, and a willingness to collaborate, you can ensure that your messages are both effective and respectful.

3. Adapting to Your Audience

Tailor your language to fit the familiarity and expectations of your audience.

The following examples illustrate how to adjust your language based on the audience you are addressing.

Example 1: Internal Team E-mail vs. E-mail to a Client

Internal Team E-mail:

"Hey team, let's get together Friday to brainstorm our next steps. Grab your coffee and be ready to throw around some ideas!"

E-mail to a Client:

"Dear [Client's Name],

We would like to schedule a meeting on Friday to discuss the next steps in our project. Your insights would be invaluable, and we look forward to collaborating closely with you."

The internal e-mail uses a casual tone appropriate for colleagues. The client e-mail, however, is more formal, reflecting professionalism and respect for the client's contribution.

Example 2: Technical Report for Specialists vs. Summary for Non-specialists

Technical Report for Specialists:

"The application of the algorithm resulted in a 15% increase in efficiency, as indicated by the quantitative analysis of the output data (refer to Table 4.3 for detailed statistical breakdown)."

Summary for Non-specialists:

"Our new method improved our system's efficiency by 15%. This means we can now do more in less time, which is great news for our project!"

The report for specialists includes technical details and jargon understood by the audience. The summary for non-specialists simplifies the language and focuses on the implications rather than the technical process.

Example 3: Social Media Update vs. Annual Report Statement

Social Media Update:

"Big news! Our team's hard work paid off, and we've seen incredible results this year. Stay tuned for what's coming next!"

Annual Report Statement:

In the past year, our dedicated team has achieved remarkable outcomes, setting the stage for further innovations and success in the upcoming period.

The social media update is informal and engaging, suitable for a broad audience and the platform's conversational style. The annual report statement is formal, reflecting the document's official and comprehensive nature.

Example 4: Presentation to Peers vs. Presentation to Executives
Presentation to Peers:

"Let's dive into how we tackled the challenges this quarter. We've got some cool insights to share, and I'm looking forward to your feedback."

Presentation to Executives:

"Today, I will outline the challenges we faced this quarter, the strategies we employed to overcome them, and the valuable insights we gained. Your feedback will be highly appreciated."

The peer presentation can afford to be more relaxed and conversational, encouraging an open dialog. The executive presentation is more structured and formal, aiming to convey respect and professionalism.

Example 5: Feedback to a New Intern vs. Feedback to a Seasoned Colleague
Feedback to a New Intern:

"You're doing a great job catching on! Let's work on developing your report-writing skills next. I have some tips that could help."

Feedback to a Seasoned Colleague:

"Your contributions continue to be invaluable. Regarding the report, I believe we can enhance its impact with some additional analysis. Let's collaborate on this."

The feedback to the intern is encouraging and instructional, recognizing his or her novice status. The feedback to the seasoned colleague is collegial and collaborative, acknowledging his or her experience and expertise.

These examples demonstrate the importance of tailoring your language to suit the familiarity and expectation of your audience, ensuring your message is both received and appreciated.

4. Avoiding Slang and Acronyms

Although slang and acronyms may make your writing more conversational, they can also make it less professional and harder to understand for a diverse audience.

The following examples show the importance of avoiding these elements for clear and professional communication.

With Slang and Acronyms	More Professional
Example 1: E-mailing a Client "Hey, just a heads-up, we need to ASAP pivot our strategy because the current one isn't cutting it. TBH, it's been a bit of a facepalm moment."	"Hello, I wanted to update you that we need to promptly adjust our strategy, as the current approach is not meeting our goals. To be honest, this has been a learning opportunity for us."
Example 2: Providing Feedback for a Team Member "Your report was OK, but IMHO, you could've gone deeper on the analysis. BTW, let's touch base IRL to discuss."	"Your report was satisfactory, but in my opinion, a more detailed analysis would have been beneficial. By the way, let's meet in person to discuss further."
Example 3: Writing a Project Update "This project is on fleek, and we're killing it with the KPIs. Gonna circle back after we dive deeper into the data."	"This project is progressing excellently, and we are exceeding our key performance indicators. I will provide another update after we have conducted a thorough analysis of the data."
Example 4: Requesting Information "Need the deets on the Q2 results ASAP. Thx."	"Could you please provide the details on the Q2 results as soon as possible? Thank you."
Example 5: Announcing a New Initiative "Excited to announce we're launching a new app that's gonna be a game-changer. It's lit!"	"We are excited to announce the launch of our new app, which we believe will significantly impact our industry."

These examples demonstrate how avoiding slang and acronyms can enhance the professionalism of your communication, making it more accessible and understandable for all readers.

Adopting a conversational but professional tone in business writing bridges the gap between clarity and formality. It humanizes business communication, making it more engaging and effective, while respecting the professional context. By following the strategies outlined above, you can enhance the ability to connect with your audience, ensuring your messages are both heard and appreciated.

Class Activity 8: *Rewrite the following sentences to make them professional but conversational.*

1. Pursuant to our discussion, it is imperative that we initiate the proposed changes posthaste.

2. Yo, can we get moving on those updates or what?

3. The undersigned requests the honor of your presence at the forthcoming quarterly review meeting.

4. Hey team, don't forget to hit up the meeting later.

5. It is of utmost importance that all employees adhere strictly to the new protocols henceforth.

3.5
Emphatic Devices in Business Writing

Emphatic devices are essential tools in business writing, enabling writers to highlight the importance of specific ideas, guide the reader's attention, and convey messages with clarity and impact. By skillfully employing these devices, writers can enhance the effectiveness of communication, ensuring that key points are noticed and remembered. This section explores various emphatic devices and how they can be applied in business writing.

3.5.1 Emphasis Through Mechanics

1. **Underlining, Italics, and Boldface**
   These are visual cues that draw people's attention to important words or

phrases. For example, using italics or boldface can highlight a new product name or a critical deadline.

2. All Capitals

Capitalizing words makes them stand out in a text, but it should be used sparingly to avoid the impression of shouting. For instance, EXPENSE-FREE immediately grabs the reader's attention.

3. Dash

Dashes can be used to add emphasis or clarify an afterthought that is significant to the main sentence.

4. Tabulation

Listing items vertically, such as in bullet points or numbered lists, can organize information clearly, and make each point stand out and easier to remember.

5. Other Means

White space, color, lines, boxes, columns, and the strategic use of titles, headings, and subheadings also serve as effective means to draw the reader's attention to important information.

3.5.2 Emphasis Through Style

1. Using Vivid and Specific Wording

Choosing concrete and specific terms over vague ones can significantly enhance the emphasis. For example, "Amway uses face-to-face selling techniques" is more impactful than "One business uses personal selling techniques."

2. Labeling the Main Idea

Clearly identifying the main idea or priority can help emphasize its importance. For instance, stating "More importantly, establish a local distribution system" makes the priority clearer.

3. Giving Important Points the Most Space

The space or detail you dedicate to a point can signal its importance. Expanding on a key argument or idea helps emphasize its significance. For instance, the original sentence goes like: "The chairperson called for a vote of the shareholders."

To emphasize the chairperson's expertise, the sentence can be expanded like:

"Having considerable experience in corporate takeover battles, the chairperson called for a vote of the shareholders."

This version highlights the chairperson's expertise upfront, adding depth and context to her actions.

Another emphasized version goes like: "The chairperson called for a vote of the shareholders. She has considerable experience in corporate takeover battles."

This version separates the details, giving the reader time to absorb the action before adding relevant background information.

4. Placing the Important Idea First or Last in the Sentence

The beginning and end of sentences are prime positions for emphasis. Placing key ideas in these spots ensures they capture the reader's attention.

For instance, the original sentence goes like: "Productivity is more likely to be increased when profit-sharing plans are linked to individual performance rather than to group performance."

To emphasize the key idea about linking profit-sharing to individual performance, the sentence can be restructured as: "Profit-sharing plans linked to individual performance rather than to group performance are more effective in increasing productivity."

This version places the key idea—individual performance—at the beginning, immediately drawing the reader's attention to the main argument.

Another emphasized version goes like: "Profit-sharing plans are more effective in increasing productivity when they are linked to individual performance rather than to group performance."

This version places the focus on the result—productivity—and concludes with the critical condition for achieving it, leaving a lasting impression.

5. Placing the Idea in a Simple Sentence or Independent Clause

Simplifying an idea by using a straightforward sentence structure or placing it in an independent clause helps maintain focus on the essential message.

For instance, the original sentence goes like: "You may take your vacuum cleaner to Ben's Appliances for repair at our expense."

To include additional context without losing focus, the sentence can be modified as: "You may take your vacuum cleaner to Ben's Appliances for repair at our expense, although it works well when it is used properly."

This version keeps the core message intact while providing additional information in a subordinate clause.

Another emphasized version goes like: "Although the vacuum cleaner works well when it is used properly, you may take your vacuum cleaner to Ben's Appliances for repair at our expense."

This version places the condition first, leading naturally to the main message about repair availability.

Another version can go like this for a slightly different emphasis: "Although you may take your vacuum cleaner to Ben's Appliances for repair at our expense, you should know it works well when it is used properly."

This version prioritizes the repair option while concluding with a note on proper usage, offering a balanced tone.

Emphatic devices, whether mechanical or stylistic, are powerful tools in business writing. They help you signal the relative importance of ideas, ensuring that critical information catches the reader's attention and is retained. By thoughtfully incorporating these devices into business documents, you can effectively guide your reader through the text, highlighting what matters most and making your communication more dynamic and persuasive.

Class Activity 9: *Rewrite the following sentences using different emphatic devices introduced in this section.*

1. We are committed to delivering quality service to our customers.

2. Meeting deadlines is crucial for the success of our projects.

3. Feedback from our clients is very important for our continuous improvement.

4. Our team has achieved significant sales growth this quarter.

5. Investing in new technology will greatly benefit our operational efficiency.

3.6
De-emphatic Devices in Business Writing

De-emphatic devices are linguistic strategies used to soften or lessen the impact of certain information in business writing. These techniques can be particularly useful when conveying sensitive or potentially negative information, allowing you to present the fact in a manner that is less likely to alarm or upset the reader.

The following shows the ways of incorporating de-emphatic devices in business communication effectively.

3.6.1 Using General Rather than Specific Wording

Generalizing information can reduce the emphasis on negative aspects or soften the delivery of potentially contentious details. For example:

- **Specific:** 125 customers complained about the issue.
- **General:** Some customers expressed concerns about the issue.

By shifting from specific to general terms, the message becomes less about the magnitude of complaints and more about acknowledging and addressing the concerns.

3.6.2 Burying the Idea in the Middle of a Sentence

Positioning a less favorable idea in the middle of a sentence, surrounded by neutral or positive information, can diminish its impact. For example:

- **Before:** The electronic parts are manufactured in Mexico, which has lower wage rates than the United States.
- **After:** Mexico, which has lower wage rates than the United States, was selected as the production site for the electronic parts.

This rearrangement makes the lower wage rates become a secondary detail rather than the main focus of the sentence.

3.6.3 Placing the Idea in a Dependent Clause Connected to an Independent Clause Containing a Positive Idea

Linking a less positive detail with a positive one in the same sentence can help offset the potential negativity. For example:

- **Less Effective:** Although items cannot be returned for cash, you will receive store credit for any returned purchases.

> • **More Effective:** You will receive store credit for any returned purchases, even though items cannot be returned for cash.

The more effective version leads with the positive aspect, ensuring that the reader's focus is on the available option rather than on the restriction.

De-emphatic devices offer a nuanced approach to conveying information that might be delicate or potentially unwelcome. By employing these techniques, business writers can communicate effectively without overshadowing messages with negativity. This approach not only maintains professionalism but also fosters a more positive relationship with the reader by ensuring that even less favorable information is delivered with care and consideration.

Class Activity 10: *Rewrite the following sentences to de-emphasize the negative aspects, applying the techniques introduced in this section.*

1. Your request for a salary increase has been denied.

2. The company will not cover relocation expenses for this position.

3. We failed to meet our sales targets this quarter.

4. The software update introduced several new bugs.

5. Employee parking will no longer be free starting next month.

Unit 4

Business Writing Strategies

Effective business writing requires more than just accurate grammar and well-chosen vocabulary; it demands a strategic approach to organize, present, and refine your content. This unit delves into essential writing strategies that will elevate your communication to new heights of clarity, impact, and professionalism. By mastering these strategies, you'll be equipped to tackle a wide range of challenges in business writing with confidence and finesse.

In the following sections, you will explore the art of organizing your writing, crafting a compelling thesis statement, using visual aids to enhance comprehension, and utilizing bullet points and lists for concise communication. As you immerse yourself in these strategies, you'll unlock the tools to craft compelling and effective business communication that captivates and convinces your readers.

4.1
Organizing Your Writing

Effective communication hinges on clear organization, which guides your readers through your content with ease and comprehension. Organizing your business writing thoughtfully can enhance its impact and allow your messages to resonate and influence. In this section, we will delve into the strategies that help you structure your content logically and create a compelling flow.

4.1.1 Why Is Organization Important?

Imagine you receive a jumbled puzzle with no clear picture. How would you feel when trying to piece it together? Similarly, disorganized writing can leave your audience feeling confused, frustrated, and less likely to engage with your messages. Here are the key reasons why organization matters.

1. **Clarity**

Proper organization clarifies messages. It helps readers follow your thoughts, understand your ideas, and grasp the intended meaning.

2. **Engagement**

Well-organized content captures your readers' attention and keeps them engaged. Readers are more likely to absorb the information when it's presented logically and coherently.

3. **Professionalism**

Organized writing reflects professionalism. It conveys that you've put thought and effort into your communication, making a positive impression on your readers.

4. **Time-Efficiency**

Organized documents save time for both the writer and the reader. Clear organization allows your readers to find the information quickly.

Class Activity 1: *Work in pairs to share some real-life examples of poorly organized documents causing confusion or misinterpretation.*

4.1.2 Methods of Organization

The effectiveness of business documents is significantly influenced by the methods of organization chosen to structure the content. The appropriate organization technique can enhance the document's clarity, persuasiveness, and user-friendliness, making it easier for your readers to follow and comprehend the information presented. This section will explore several key methods of organization that are instrumental in crafting coherent and impactful business documents, and discuss the benefits and applications of chronological order, spatial order, order of importance, problem-solution method, and cause-and-effect method, among others. Each method offers distinct advantages depending on the document's purpose, the nature of the information, and the intended audience. Understanding these methods will equip you with the tools to select the most effective approach for organizing your content, thereby improving the efficiency of your communication.

1. Chronological Order

It means to present the information in a time-based sequence. This is useful for explaining events, processes, or project timelines. For example:

Scenario: Writing a Project Progress Report

Subject: Project Progress Report—Q3 Marketing Campaign

Dear Team,

I am pleased to provide an update on the progress of our Q3 marketing campaign, which commenced on July 1st and will conclude on September 30th. This report outlines the key milestones and achievements we've reached in chronological order.

1. Campaign Kick-Off (July 1–7):
   - During the first week of July, our marketing team assembled to launch the campaign officially.
   - All team members received comprehensive briefs and clarified their roles.
2. Content Creation (July 8–21):
   - Over the next two weeks, our content team focused on creating engaging content for social media platforms and e-mail marketing.
   - A content calendar was established to maintain consistency.
3. Social Media Promotion (July 22–31):
   - Starting in late July, we began rolling out our campaign on various social media platforms.
   - Engagements and reach steadily increased during this period.
4. E-mail Marketing (August 1–15):
   - In early August, we initiated our e-mail marketing efforts, targeting our subscriber list.
   - Open rates and click-through rates exceeded our expectations.
5. Mid-campaign Review (August 16):
   - On August 16th, we conducted a mid-campaign review to assess performance against our initial goals.
   - Adjustments were made to maximize our impact.
6. Continued Promotion (August 17–September 29):
   - The remainder of August and September saw continued promotional activities.

- We closely monitored performance metrics and made real-time adjustments to optimize results.

7. Campaign Wrap-Up (September 30):

- On September 30th, we concluded the campaign and began compiling data for a comprehensive analysis.
- Preliminary results indicated a significant increase in brand visibility and engagement.

In conclusion, our Q3 marketing campaign proceeded in chronological order, allowing us to track progress and make timely adjustments. The success we've achieved so far is a testament to our team's dedication and effective planning.

Best Regards,

[Your Name]

Marketing Manager

In this example, the writer uses chronological order to present the progress of a marketing campaign. Each section is organized by the time frame in which activities occurred, providing a clear and structured overview of the campaign's development. This approach helps readers follow the sequence of events and understand the project's timeline and achievements clearly.

2. Spatial Order

It means to arrange details based on the physical or geographical layout. This is useful for explaining location-based descriptions, facility layouts, or physical objects. For example:

Subject: Introduction to Our New Office Layout

Dear Team,

As we prepare to move into our new office space next week, I want to give you a detailed walkthrough of the layout, arranged for maximum efficiency and comfort. The new office is designed with a spatial arrangement that reflects our dynamic work culture and collaborative spirit.

Entrance and Reception Area: As you enter the office, you'll be greeted by a spacious reception area. To the left of the entrance, we have our reception desk, which will be staffed by our friendly administrative team. The waiting area for visitors is furnished with comfortable seating and a selection of magazines.

Main Workspace: Directly behind the reception area is the main open-plan workspace. This large area is divided into four quadrants, each assigned to different departments. The quadrants are separated by low partitions, allowing for easy communication and collaboration. Each workstation is equipped with ergonomic chairs and adjustable desks.

Meeting Rooms and Manager Offices: To the right of the main workspace, you'll find a series of glass-walled meeting rooms. Each room is equipped with video conferencing facilities and presentation tools. Alongside the meeting rooms are the offices for department managers, allowing for easy access and visibility.

Break Room and Kitchenette: At the far end of the office, adjacent to the main workspace, is our new break room and kitchenette. This area features modern appliances, a coffee machine, and a comfortable lounge area for relaxation and informal meetings.

Training and Conference Hall: To the left of the main workspace is a large training and conference hall. This multifunctional space is designed for larger meetings, training sessions, and company-wide gatherings. It's equipped with advanced audio-visual technology for presentations and events.

Restrooms and Utility Areas: Restrooms are conveniently located at the opposite ends of the office space, near the break room and reception area. Additionally, utility areas with office supplies and printing stations are situated in each quadrant of the main workspace for easy accessibility.

We believe this spatial layout will not only enhance our work efficiency but also create a more enjoyable and collaborative work environment. We look forward to seeing you all settle into this new space and bring it to life with your energy and creativity.

Best regards,

[Your Name]

[Your Position]

In this example, spatial order is used to describe the physical layout of the new office. It guides readers through the office space, moving from one physical location to another in a logical order. This approach is particularly useful for helping the team visualize the new environment and understand the arrangement of different areas within the office.

3. Order of Importance

It means to start with the most critical information and work the way down. This is useful for highlighting key points or prioritizing items. For example:

Subject: Project Falcon—Urgent Status Update

Dear Stakeholders,

I am writing to provide an urgent update on Project Falcon. This message outlines critical issues that require immediate attention, followed by developments of lesser urgency but significant impact. Your prompt response to these points will be greatly appreciated.

Critical Delay in Software Development (High Priority): Our top concern is a two-week delay in the software development phase due to unforeseen technical challenges. This setback impacts our project timeline significantly. Immediate action is required to reallocate resources and adjust our schedule to mitigate further delays.

Budget Overrun in Marketing (Medium Priority): The marketing department has reported a 15% overrun in the allocated budget. While this does not halt current operations, it necessitates a review of our spending and reallocation of funds to ensure financial stability for the project's remaining phases.

Vendor Contract Renewal (Lower Priority): Our contract with the current software vendor is due for renewal in 60 days. While not immediate, early renegotiation is advised to secure favorable terms and avoid service disruption.

Successful Pilot Testing (Informational): On a positive note, our recent pilot testing of the new system was successful, demonstrating robust performance and user satisfaction. This milestone, while less urgent, is crucial for stakeholder confidence and project momentum.

Next Steps and Call to Action: To address these issues, we propose an emergency meeting of key project leaders and stakeholders. Our goal is to formulate a strategic plan to tackle the software development delay and budget overrun, ensuring minimal impact on the project's final delivery.

Your input and decision-making are crucial at this juncture. Please confirm your availability for the proposed meeting or suggest alternate timings. We appreciate your continued support and commitment to making Project Falcon a success.

Best regards,

[Your Name]

[Project Manager]

In this example, the order of importance is used to structure the update, starting with the most critical issue (the delay in software development) and ending with less urgent but still relevant information (successful pilot testing). This approach ensures that the most pressing concerns are addressed first, capturing readers' attention and prioritizing the action.

4. Problem-Solution Method

It means to begin by identifying a problem or challenge, and then present solutions. This is useful for explaining proposals, business plans, and issue-focused documents. For example:

Subject: Proposal to Enhance Customer Service Efficiency

Dear Management Team,

Problem Identification

Recent customer feedback and our internal reviews have identified a significant challenge in our customer service department: extended wait times and delayed responses. This issue has led to customer dissatisfaction and a decline in service quality ratings. Our analysis indicates that the primary cause is the current manual ticketing system, which is inefficient and prone to errors.

Proposed Solution

To address this critical issue, I propose the implementation of an automated customer service system. The solution involves two key components:

Integration of an AI-Powered Chatbot: The chatbot will handle initial customer inquiries, providing instant responses to common questions. This will reduce the workload on human agents and ensure customers receive immediate assistance for straightforward issues.

Adoption of an Advanced Ticketing System: The new system will automatically categorize and assign tickets based on query types and complexity. This will streamline the process, reduce response times, and enhance the efficiency of our customer service team.

Benefits:

- Improved Customer Satisfaction: Quicker response times and efficient query handling will enhance the overall customer experience.
- Increased Efficiency: Automation will free up our team to focus on more complex queries, thereby increasing productivity.
- Data-driven Insights: The system will provide valuable data on customer queries and service metrics, aiding in continuous improvement.

Implementation Plan:

We propose a phased implementation, starting with a pilot program in one department. Post successful pilot results, we will roll out the system across all customer service departments. Training sessions will be conducted to ensure our team is well-equipped to use the new system.

Conclusion:

This proposal offers a practical solution to our current customer service challenges. By embracing technology, we can significantly improve our service quality and enhance customer satisfaction. We are confident that this investment will yield substantial returns in terms of customer loyalty and brand reputation.

I look forward to discussing this proposal further and am available for any questions or additional information.

Best Regards,

[Your Name]

[Your Position]

In this example, the problem-solution method clearly outlines a significant issue affecting the company and then provides a detailed solution to address it. This approach is effective for proposing changes or improvements, as it directly links the need for action with a practical and clear plan to resolve the issue.

5. Cause-and-Effect Method

It means to show the relationship between causes and their effects. This is useful for analyzing situations, discussing consequences, or explaining why something happened. For example:

Subject: Analysis Report on Q2 Sales Decline

Dear Board Members,

This report aims to provide an in-depth analysis of the causes leading with the decline in sales during the second quarter (Q2) and the subsequent effects on our company's overall performance.

Cause: Increased Competition in the Market

Effect: Our market share has been impacted due to new entrants in the market offering similar products at competitive prices. This has led to a noticeable shift in customer preferences and a 15% decrease in our sales volume compared with the previous quarter.

Cause: Supply Chain Disruptions

Effect: Unforeseen disruptions in our supply chain, primarily due to global shipping delays, resulted in stock shortages of key products. This caused an inability to meet customer demand promptly, contributing to a 10% decline in sales revenue.

Cause: Changes in Consumer Buying Behavior

Effect: A shift in consumer behavior towards online shopping has been observed, with a significant portion of our traditional customer base moving to digital platforms. Our limited online presence has resulted in a loss of sales opportunities, particularly in the younger demographic segment.

Cause: Lack of Product Innovation

Effect: A stagnant product line without significant innovations or updates has led to reduced interest from our existing customers. This has not only affected repeat purchases but also hindered attracting new customers, causing a cumulative sales drop of approximately 8%.

Conclusion and Recommendations:

The decline in sales is a multifaceted issue, primarily driven by increased competition, supply chain disruptions, changing consumer behavior, and our current product offerings. To address these challenges, I recommend the following actions:

- Competitive Analysis and Pricing Strategy: conduct a thorough competitive analysis and adjust our pricing strategy to offer more value to our customers;
- Strengthen Supply Chain Resilience: work on diversifying our supplier base and optimizing inventory management to mitigate future disruptions;
- Enhance Online Presence: invest in expanding our digital footprint, including an e-commerce platform and digital marketing strategies;
- Focus on Product Innovation: initiate a product development plan to introduce new and updated products that meet changing market needs.

Addressing these causes effectively will help in reversing the sales decline and position our company for future growth. I look forward to discussing these recommendations in our upcoming meeting.

Sincerely,

[Your Name]

[Your Position]

In this example, the cause-and-effect method is used to analyze the recent decline in sales by identifying specific causes and explaining their direct impact on

商务英语写作实用教程
Business English Writing: A Practical Course

the company's sales performance. This approach is effective for providing a clear understanding of the issues and guiding the development of strategies to address them.

Class Activity 2: *Write one of the business documents according to the required method of organization.*

1. Chronological Order

    Objective: Write a brief e-mail about the project update to your team, organizing the information in chronological order from the project's start to the current status.

2. Order of Importance

    Objective: Draft a proposal for a new company initiative. Begin with the most compelling argument or benefit to the company, and follow with supporting arguments in descending order of importance.

3. Problem-Solution Method

    Objective: Compose a memo addressing a current challenge within your department. Clearly define the problem and follow with a detailed solution that addresses it.

4.2
Crafting a Strong Thesis Statement

A strong thesis statement is the foundation of any well-structured piece of writing. It serves as a roadmap, guiding your readers through the main points of your content. This section explores the significance of crafting a robust thesis statement and provides guidance on creating one that effectively communicates your central message.

4.2.1 Understanding the Components of a Thesis Statement

A thesis statement is a concise declaration of the main point or argument you're making in your writing. It encapsulates the essence of your message and gives your readers a clear sense of what to expect. In business English writing, a thesis statement serves as a compass for your document, guiding the readers through your arguments and ideas. It is especially crucial in business contexts, where clarity and precision are paramount. The following will explore the three key components that make a thesis statement effective in a business writing context.

1. Clear and Concise Subject (Topic)

A thesis statement in business writing must clearly state the central idea or argument. It should be specific enough to provide a clear direction for the document while maintaining a focus on a particular aspect of the business topic. For example:

> - **Implementing remote work policies in small businesses** can enhance productivity and employee satisfaction, as evidenced by reduced overhead costs and improved work-life balance:

2. Assertive Stance or Argument

A thesis statement in business writing should assert a clear, strong stance or perspective. This assertiveness helps set the tone for the document and indicate a confident approach to the subject matter. For example:

> - Investing in sustainable practices is **not only ethically imperative but also economically beneficial for long-term corporate growth.**

3. Outline of Supporting Points

A thesis statement should briefly outline the key points or arguments that will be developed in the document. This component helps structure the document and guides the readers through the logical progression of the argument. For example:

> - The adoption of digital transformation in retail banking, **through mobile banking, online services, and AI-driven customer support**, is essential for staying competitive in the rapidly evolving financial sector.

The thesis statement in business English writing should be a clear, assertive, and well-focused sentence that provides a roadmap for the document. It must convey the main idea, assert a stance, and briefly outline the supporting arguments or points. A well-crafted thesis statement sets the tone for the document, ensuring that the message is delivered effectively and efficiently to the business audience.

Class Activity 3: *Analyze the components of the following thesis statements in business English writing and underline the topic, the assertive stance or argument, and the outline of supporting points with different marks.*

1. Business Report on Market Expansion

   Thesis Statement: "Expanding our presence into emerging markets is a strategic move because it offers substantial growth opportunities and diversifies our revenue streams."

2. Marketing E-mail for a New Product Launch

   Thesis Statement: "Our new product, XYZ, will revolutionize the market by addressing a critical consumer need for sustainable and cost-effective solutions."

3. Persuasive Proposal for Employee Training

   Thesis Statement: "Implementing a comprehensive employee training program is essential to enhance staff productivity, improve job satisfaction, and reduce turnover."

4.2.2 How to Craft an Effective Thesis Statement

Be Clear and Specific: Your thesis statement should convey a specific idea, avoiding vague or general statements.

Express a Controllable Idea: Your thesis statement should focus on aspects that can be discussed and supported within your writing.

Reflect Your Main Points: Your thesis statement should provide a roadmap for your content, indicating the main points or arguments you'll address.

Avoid Ambiguity: Your thesis statement should stay away from vague language that might confuse your readers.

Consider Your Audience: Your should tailor your thesis statement to your audience's level of understanding and familiarity with the topic.

The following are some examples of strong thesis statements:

- This report examines the impact of solar energy adoption on residential electricity consumption, highlighting its potential to reduce carbon emissions.
- This proposal advocates for the implementation of a remote work policy to enhance employee productivity, work-life balance, and overall job satisfaction.

- This manual provides step-by-step instructions for assembling our innovative home fitness equipment, ensuring a safe and effective workout experience.

These thesis statements provide clear and specific arguments or points of view that can be debated or supported by the rest of the writing. They also convey the main purpose and focus of the writing, making it easier for readers to understand and engage with the content.

Class Activity 4: *Read the following various business scenarios and topics, and practice your skills in crafting thesis statements.*

1. Scenario: You work for a tech start-up, and need to write a proposal to secure funding for developing a new mobile app.

   Topic: Funding a New Mobile App

   Thesis Statement: _____

   _____

2. Scenario: You're a marketing manager tasked with creating a marketing plan for launching a new line of sustainable, eco-friendly products.

   Topic: Marketing Strategy for Sustainable Products

   Thesis Statement: _____

   _____

3. Scenario: You've been asked to write an e-mail to your team about the upcoming company-wide training session on cybersecurity.

   Topic: Company-Wide Cybersecurity Training

   Thesis Statement: _____

   _____

4. Scenario: You're a sales executive crafting an e-mail to potential clients to introduce your company's new software product.

   Topic: Introducing New Software Product

   Thesis Statement: _____

   _____

Class Activity 5: *Work in pairs or groups to revise the following weak thesis statement to make it more effective and clearly state the purpose and benefits of the proposed program.*

Topic: Project Proposal for Employee Wellness Program

Weak Thesis Statement: We should consider implementing an employee wellness program because it's a good idea.

4.3
Using Visual Aids

In today's fast-paced business environment, the ability to communicate complex information quickly and clearly is invaluable. The use of visuals in business documents, from reports to presentations, can transform the way information is perceived and processed. Diagrams, charts, graphs, and other visual aids can break down complex data, highlight trends, and illustrate relationships in a way that text alone cannot. However, the effectiveness of these tools hinges on their proper creation and integration. This section will guide you through the various types of diagrams and visual representations commonly used in business English writing. It will provide insights on when and how to use these tools to convey your messages effectively. You'll learn about the principles of design and clarity, ensuring that your visuals complement your written content, rather than overshadow it. Whether you're preparing a detailed report, a persuasive proposal, or an impactful presentation, understanding how to effectively use visual aids can be a game-changer.

4.3.1 Importance of Visual Elements in Business Writing

In business English writing, visual elements are not merely decorative; they are a crucial component of effective communication. This section will explore the significance of incorporating visual elements into business documents and presentations, underlining their role in enhancing comprehension, improving engagement and communication effectiveness, and facilitating cross-cultural communication.

1. **Enhancing Comprehension**

Simplifying Complex Information: Visuals can distill complex data and concepts into more digestible formats, making it easier for the audience to understand and analyze critical information.

Facilitating Quick Analysis: In a business setting where time is often a constraint, visuals allow for rapid data analysis and decision-making. Graphs and charts, for instance, can convey trends and comparisons at a glance.

Aiding Memory Retention: Visual elements are more likely to be remembered than text alone. This is particularly important in business writing where key points and data need to be recalled for decision-making.

2. Improving Engagement

Attracting Attention: A document or presentation with well-designed visuals is more engaging and can hold the audience's attention longer than text-heavy content.

Breaking Monotony: Visuals break up long stretches of text, making the content more readable and less intimidating.

3. Improving Communication Effectiveness

Supporting Persuasion: Well-chosen visuals can be persuasive tools. For instance, a graph showing the growth potential of a project can support a business proposal more effectively than text alone.

Enhancing Credibility: Professional and accurate visual representations can enhance the credibility of the writer or presenter, demonstrating a thorough analysis of the data.

4. Facilitating Cross-Cultural Communication

Transcending Language Barriers: Visuals can be understood across languages and cultures, making them indispensable in global business communication.

Catering to Diverse Learning Styles: Different people absorb information differently. Visuals cater to visual learners and complement auditory and kinesthetic learning styles.

The use of visual elements in business writing is not just a matter of aesthetic preference; it's a strategic tool for effective communication. By simplifying complex data, enhancing engagement, improving communication effectiveness, and facilitating cross-cultural communication, visuals serve a pivotal role in the business environment. As we move forward in this digital and data-driven age, the ability to integrate visuals into business writing becomes increasingly vital.

Class Activity 6: *The following are two versions of a business document: One is text-only and the other is integrated with visual elements. Work in groups to compare the two versions and discuss how visuals affect readers' understanding and interest. Each group presents their findings, focusing on the importance of visual elements in business communication.*

Topic for Business Report: Annual Sales Analysis

Version 1:

Introduction

The purpose of this report is to analyze the annual sales performance of our company for the fiscal year 2023. This analysis covers various product lines and regional sales performances to identify trends, opportunities for growth, and areas requiring improvement.

Sales Performance Overview

In 2023, the company's total sales revenue was $10 million, representing a 5% increase compared with the previous year. The most significant growth was observed in the electronics division, which saw a 10% increase in sales, amounting to $4 million. Conversely, the home appliances division experienced a slight decline of 2%, resulting in sales of $2 million.

Regional Sales Analysis

The North American market contributed 50% of the total sales revenue, followed by Europe at 30%, and Asia at 20%. Notably, sales in the Asian market increased by 8%, indicating a growing presence in this region.

Conclusion

The overall sales performance of the company in 2023 was positive, with significant growth in the electronics division and the Asian market. However, efforts need to be made to address the decline in the home appliances division.

Version 2:

Introduction

The purpose of this report is to analyze the annual sales performance of our company for the fiscal year 2023. This analysis covers various product lines and regional sales performances to identify trends, opportunities for growth, and areas requiring improvement.

Sales Performance Overview

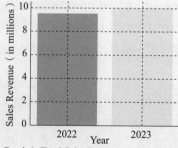

Graph 1: Total Sales Revenue 2022 vs. 2023

The bar graph shows a 5% increase in total sales revenue, with 2023 sales at $10 million compared with $9.5 million in 2022.

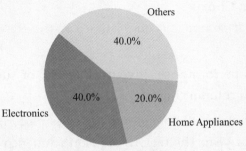

Graph 2: Sales by Division

The pie chart illustrates sales distribution: Electronics 40%, Home Appliances 20%, and Others 40%.

Regional Sales Analysis

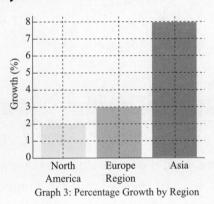

Graph 3: Percentage Growth by Region

The bar graph displays growth rates: North America (+2%), Europe (+3%), and Asia (+8%).

Conclusion

The overall sales performance of the company in 2023 was positive, with significant growth in the electronics division and the Asian market. However, efforts need to be made to address the decline in the home appliances division.

4.3.2 Types of Diagrams in Business Contexts

Diagrams are a cornerstone of visual communication in business contexts. They are helpful in representing data, explaining processes, and visualizing relationships in a clear and concise manner. This section will explore various types of diagrams commonly used in business contexts and their specific applications.

1. Bar and Column Charts

Purpose: Ideal for comparing quantities across different categories or time periods.

Use Cases: Sales performance, inventory levels, or survey results are often depicted using bar and column charts.

Suppose a company wants to compare its sales performance across different regions for a particular year. The regions are North America ($1.2 million), Europe ($900,000), Asia ($1.5 million), and South America ($700,000). The following is a bar chart depicting the sales performance across different regions.

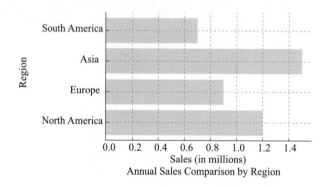

Annual Sales Comparison by Region

In the bar chart above, each region would be represented on the Y-axis (vertical axis), and the sales figures would be represented on the X-axis (horizontal axis). Each bar's length would correspond to the sales figures, allowing for a clear comparison across regions.

Here is another example. A business wants to track its customer acquisition over the months of a year.

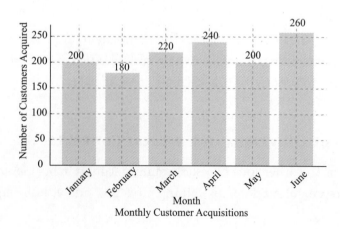

Monthly Customer Acquisitions

In the column chart above, each month would be represented on the X-axis, and the number of customers acquired would be on the Y-axis. Each column's height would correspond to the number of customers acquired in that month, providing a visual representation of trends and variations over the year.

2. Line Graphs

Purpose: Best suited for displaying data trends over time.

Use Cases: Commonly used to show revenue growth, website traffic trends, or market changes.

Suppose a company wants to track its revenue growth each quarter over a period of two years. The following is the line chart for the company's quarterly revenue growth over two years.

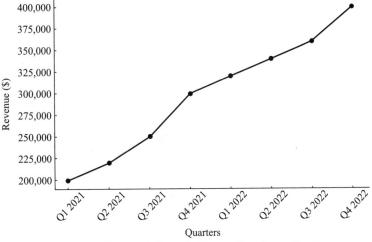

Company's Quarterly Revenue Growth over Two Years

In the line chart above, the X-axis represents the time period, breaking down into quarters (Q1 2021, Q2 2021, ..., Q4 2022), and the Y-axis represents the company's revenue in dollars. Each point on the chart corresponds to the company's revenue at the end of each quarter. A line is drawn connecting these points, showing the trend of the company's revenue over the two-year period. This line chart would visually depict the company's revenue growth trend, making it easy to see any increases or decreases in revenue at a glance. It's particularly useful for identifying patterns or trends over time, such as seasonal fluctuations or consistent growth.

3. Pie Charts

Purpose: Effective for showing the composition or proportional distribution of data.

Use Cases: Market share, budget allocations, or customer segmentation are typically represented using pie charts.

Suppose a company has a total marketing budget of $100,000 for the year and it's allocated across various channels. The following is the pie chart for the company's marketing budget allocation.

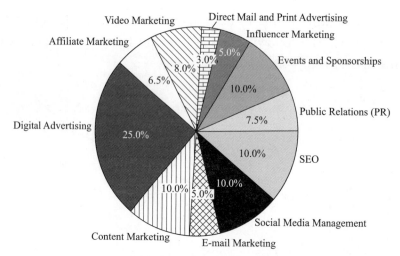

Marketing Budget Allocation ($100,000)

In the pie chart above, each slice of the pie represents a different marketing channel. The size of each slice is proportional to the amount of budget allocated to that channel. For instance, the slice for Digital Advertising, which has the largest allocation ($25,000), would be the largest of the pie. The pie chart would visually depict how the total marketing budget is divided, making it easy to see which channels are receiving more or less investment. This type of pie chart is useful for quickly understanding how a budget is distributed across various categories, and for making comparisons between them. It's a common tool used in presentations and reports to summarize financial allocations, market share, survey results, and more.

4. Flowcharts

Purpose: Useful for outlining processes or workflows.

Use Cases: Demonstrating decision-making processes, project stages, or operational workflows.

The following is an example flowchart for handling customer complaints.

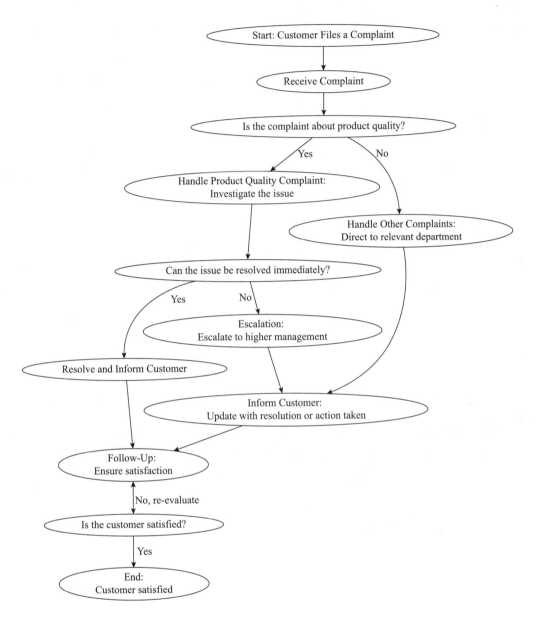

Customer Complaint Handling Process

5. Gantt Charts

Purpose: Primarily used for project management to showcase timelines and task progress.

Use Cases: Planning and tracking project timelines, milestones, and dependencies.

A Gantt chart is a type of bar chart that illustrates a project schedule. It's a useful tool in project management for showing the start and finish dates of various elements of a project. Let's consider an example of a Gantt chart for a simple project:

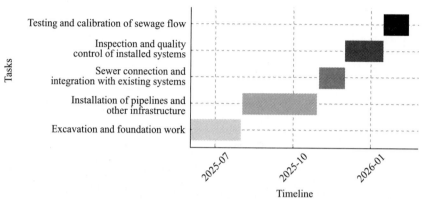

Gantt Chart for Construction Stage of the Sewage Diversion Renovation Project

Project: Sewage Diversion Renovation

In the Gantt chart above, each of these phases would be represented as a horizontal bar spanning the start date to the end date. The chart provides a clear visual timeline of the project, showing when each phase starts, how long it is expected to take, and where activities overlap. It's an effective way to view the entire project timeline at a glance and to track progress throughout the project lifecycle.

6. Scatter Plots

Purpose: Ideal for identifying correlations or patterns between two variables.

Use Cases: Used in data analysis to spot trends, or potential correlations in datasets.

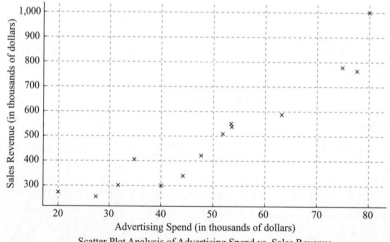

Scatter Plot Analysis of Advertising Spend vs. Sales Revenue

To understand the effectiveness of the advertising efforts, a company conducted an analysis to explore the relationship between advertising spend and sales revenue. The report utilizes a scatter plot to visually represent this relationship, aiming to identify patterns and potential areas for optimization. The scatter plot displays data points for each month over the past year. The horizontal axis (X-axis) represents the advertising spend (in thousands of dollars), while the vertical axis (Y-axis) represents the sales revenue generated (in thousands of dollars). Each point on the scatter plot corresponds to a month's performance, allowing them to observe how changes in advertising spend are associated with variations in sales revenue.

7. Venn Diagrams

Purpose: Excellent for showing relationships and intersections between different sets of data.

Use Cases: Market analysis, product comparisons, or identifying common traits among different customer segments.

A Venn diagram is a graphical representation used to show the relationships between different sets. It typically consists of overlapping circles, where each circle represents a set, and the overlap between circles represents the common elements of those sets. Let's consider an example of a Venn diagram.

Imagine we have three different dietary groups: vegetarians, gluten-free dieters, and nut allergy sufferers. We want to illustrate the overlap in food choices among these groups: Circle 1: vegetarians (foods that don't include meat or fish); Circle 2: gluten-free dieters (foods without gluten); Circle 3: nut allergy sufferers (foods that don't contain nuts).

In the Venn diagram, the area where Circle 1 and Circle 2 overlap shows foods that are both vegetarian and gluten-free. The area where Circle 2 and Circle 3 overlap indicates foods that are both gluten-free and nut-free. The area where Circle 1 and Circle 3 overlap represents foods that are both vegetarian and nut-free. The central area where all three circles overlap would represent foods that are vegetarian, gluten-free, and nut-free.

The Venn diagram on the next page would visually depict the commonalities and differences in food choices between these three dietary groups, making it easier to understand the potential dietary options that cater to all three groups.

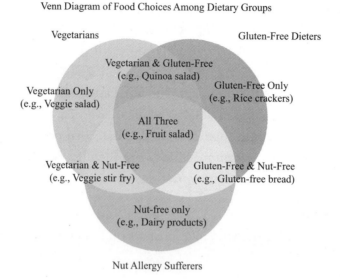

Venn Diagram of Food Choices Among Dietary Groups

8. Radar Charts

Use: Useful for comparing multiple variables.

Example: Comparing the performance of different employees across various parameters.

Features: A circular chart with spokes, each representing one axis of the data.

In a business context, a radar chart is an excellent visual tool for comparing multiple variables across different entities, such as products, services, or performance metrics. Here's an example of how a radar chart can be integrated into business writing, focusing on product comparison across various features.

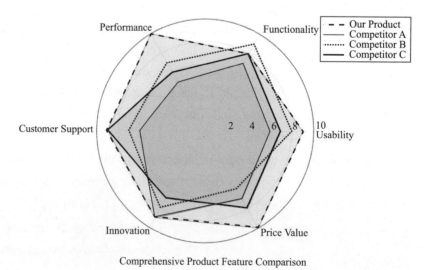

Comprehensive Product Feature Comparison

To continuously improve product offerings and better meet market demands, we have conducted a detailed comparison of our flagship product against the leading competitors in the market. This analysis employs a radar chart to visually represent and compare the performance of each product across six key features: usability, functionality, performance, customer support, innovation, and price value.

The radar chart presents a six-axis graph, where each axis represents one of the key features mentioned above. The scale for each feature is standardized to facilitate an equitable comparison. Our product and each of the competitors are represented by distinct lines that span across these axes, forming polygons that visually encapsulate the performance profile of each product.

Using a radar chart in this manner helps stakeholders quickly grasp comparative strengths and weaknesses, guiding strategic discussions and decision-making processes in product development, marketing, and competitive strategy.

Each of these charts and graphs serves a specific purpose and can be selected based on the type of data and the message you wish to convey. Effectively used, they can transform complex data into easily digestible and actionable information.

The choice of diagram in a business context depends on the type of information being conveyed and the intended message. Each type of diagram has its unique strengths and is best suited for specific kinds of data representation. Understanding how to use these diagrams effectively can significantly enhance the clarity and impact of business communication.

4.3.3 Creating Clear and Effective Diagrams

Creating clear and effective diagrams is essential in conveying information accurately and efficiently in business communication. This section provides insights into the key principles of diagram design to enhance clarity and effectiveness.

1. **Clarity and Simplicity**
   Simplify Complex Information: Break down complex data into simpler, more digestible visual forms. Avoid overcrowding the diagram with too much information.

   Focus on Key Data: Emphasize the most important information. Use visual hierarchies, like varying sizes or colors, to highlight key points.

2. **Consistency in Design**
   Uniform Style: Maintain a consistent style throughout your diagrams. This

includes using uniform fonts, colors, and line styles.

Repetitive Elements: Use similar shapes, colors, and icons to represent the same type of information across different diagrams.

3. Use of Color

Color for Emphasis: Use color strategically to draw the audience's attention to important areas or to distinguish different data sets.

Color Harmony: Choose colors that are visually pleasing and provide sufficient contrast. Be mindful of colorblind-friendly palettes.

4. Labeling and Typography

Clear Labels: Ensure all parts of the diagram are clearly labeled. Use legible font sizes and styles.

Minimal Text: Use text sparingly. Rely more on visual elements to convey information. When text is necessary, keep it concise.

5. Scale and Proportions

Accurate Scaling: Ensure that the scales used in diagrams (like in bar graphs or line charts) are accurate and proportionate, to avoid misleading representation.

Proportional Representation: In diagrams like pie charts, ensure that proportions accurately reflect the data.

6. Accessibility

Readable Formats: Make sure diagrams are readable in various formats, including print and digital.

Accessibility for All: Consider visual impairments; use alternative text descriptions for crucial visual elements.

7. Integration with Text

Contextual Placement: Place diagrams close to the relevant text in your document.

Reference in Text: When you introduce a diagram, reference it in the text to guide the readers.

Effective diagrams are not just visually appealing; they are tools for better communication. By adhering to the principles of clarity, consistency, effective use of color, appropriate labeling, and scale accuracy, you can create diagrams that not only capture the audience's attention but also aid in the comprehension of complex information. Remember, a well-designed diagram can significantly enhance the effectiveness of your business communication.

4.3.4 Integrating Diagrams with Text

The integration of diagrams with text in business writing is a critical aspect of effective communication. Diagrams can complement and enhance the understanding of the textual content, but only if they are seamlessly integrated. This section focuses on the best practices for combining diagrams with text to create cohesive and informative business documents.

1. **Placement and Relevance**

    Strategic Placement: Position diagrams near the related text to ensure the readers can easily make connections between the visual and written information.

    Relevance: Ensure that each diagram directly relates to the accompanying text and adds value to it. Avoid using visuals that don't support or clarify the text.

2. **Referencing Diagrams in Text**

    Clear References: When introducing a diagram, refer to it explicitly in your text (e.g., "As shown in Figure 1..."). This guides the readers to the visual and emphasizes its importance.

    Descriptive Captions: Provide captions that not only label the diagram (e.g., "Figure 1: Annual sales growth") but also briefly explain what it represents or highlights.

3. **Consistency in Presentation**

    Uniform Style Across Document: Maintain a consistent style for diagrams throughout the document. This includes using similar fonts, colors, and line styles as used in the text.

    Alignment with Document Format: Ensure that the size and orientation of diagrams fit well within the overall layout of the document.

4. **Enhancing Comprehension**

    Supplementary Role: Use diagrams to supplement the text, not to replace it. The visual should add a layer of understanding or provide an example of what is discussed in the text.

    Progressive Disclosure: Introduce more complex diagrams progressively. Start with basic visuals and gradually move to more detailed ones as the text delves deeper into the topic.

5. Accessibility and Inclusivity

Alt Text for Diagrams: Include alternative text descriptions for diagrams to ensure accessibility for the readers using screen readers or those with visual impairments.

Consideration for Print and Digital Formats: Be aware of how diagrams will appear in different formats, such as printed documents versus online content.

6. Balancing Text and Visuals

Avoid Overcrowding: While diagrams are valuable, too many visuals can overwhelm the readers. Strike a balance between text and diagrams.

Complementary Information: Ensure that diagrams and text complement each other and that the information is not redundant.

Integrating diagrams with text in business writing, when done effectively, can greatly enhance the readers' comprehension and engagement. It's about finding the right balance and ensuring that each visual element is purposeful and enhances the narrative of the text. By following these guidelines, you can create documents that are not only informative but also visually appealing and accessible to a broad audience.

Class Activity 7: *Write an explanatory text for the following diagram.*

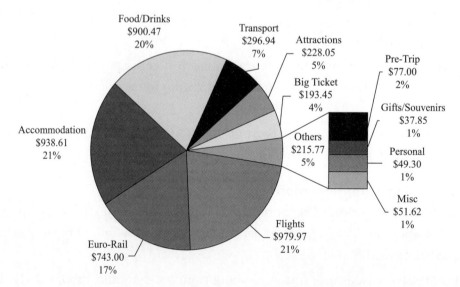

Total Expenses by Category

4.3.5 Writing for the Diagrams

1. Structuring Written Summaries (Introduction, Body, and Conclusion)

Structuring written summaries effectively is crucial for clarity and coherence. A well-structured summary should have an introduction, body, and conclusion.

1) Introduction

The introduction sets the context for the readers. It typically includes the title of the chart or graph, the source of the data (if available), what the chart or graph represents, the time period or the data range, and the units of measurement. For example:

> The provided bar chart, sourced from the Annual Environmental Report 2012, illustrates the recycling rates of four materials: paper, glass, aluminum, and plastic, in the United States from 1982 to 2010. Data is presented as a percentage of total waste recycled annually.

2) Body

The body of the summary is where the main information is conveyed. It should describe significant trends (increases, decreases, fluctuations); compare data points, if relevant (e.g., one category against another); highlight any notable data points (peaks, troughs, anomalies); and avoid interpreting or adding information not present in the chart. For example:

> Over the decade, paper consistently showed the highest recycling rate, peaking at 80% in 1994. Glass recycling rates also increased but remained significantly lower, hovering around 60% by 2010. Aluminum displayed a steady growth, rising from 5% to 45% by the end of the period. Plastic, despite starting at the lowest rate of 4% in 1990, saw a gradual increase, reaching 10% in 2010. The most notable change was observed in aluminum recycling rates, which tripled from 1994 to 2010 and maintained an upward trajectory.

3) Conclusion

The conclusion should summarize the key points and possibly suggest implications or a brief explanation of the trends, without introducing new information. It should restate the main trend or finding; summarize how the data has changed over time;

and optionally, suggest possible reasons for the trends if the chart provides such information. For example:

In conclusion, the chart demonstrates a positive trend in recycling rates across all materials from 1982 to 2010. Paper recycling remained predominant throughout the decade, while plastic showed the most significant percentage increase. The data reflects a growing environmental awareness and the impact of recycling initiatives.

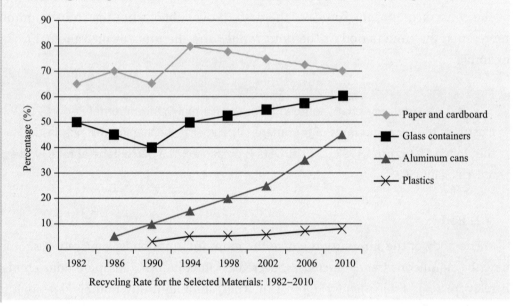

Recycling Rate for the Selected Materials: 1982–2010

The following is a full summary example:

The provided bar chart, sourced from the Annual Environmental Report 2023, illustrates the recycling rates of four materials: paper, glass, aluminum, and plastic, in the United States from 1982 to 2010. Data is presented as a percentage of total waste recycled annually. Over the decade, paper consistently showed the highest recycling rate, peaking at 80% in 1994. Glass recycling rates also increased but remained significantly lower, hovering around 60% by 2010. Aluminum displayed a steady growth, rising from 5% to 45% by the end of the period. Plastic, despite starting at the lowest rate of 4% in 1990, saw a gradual increase, reaching around 10% in 2010. The most notable change was observed in aluminum recycling rates, which tripled from 1994 to 2010 and maintained an upward trajectory. In conclusion, the chart demonstrates a positive trend in recycling rates across all materials from 1982 to 2010.

Paper recycling remained predominant throughout the decade, while plastic showed the most significant percentage increase. The data reflects a growing environmental awareness and the impact of recycling initiatives.

Another full summary version of the same diagram is shown as follows:

The line graph provides data on the recycling rates of four different materials—paper and cardboard, glass containers, aluminum cans, and plastics—over approximately three decades, from 1982 to 2010.

From an overall perspective, paper and cardboard consistently had the highest recycling rates among the materials shown, starting from just above 60% in 1982 and peaking close to 80% in the late 1990s before experiencing a slight decline to just below 70% by 2010. Glass containers, the second most recycled material, demonstrated a gradual increase in its recycling rate from just over 50% in 1982 to approximately 60% in 2010.

Aluminum cans saw a significant rise in recycling rates throughout the period, starting from under 10% in 1982 and increasing to around 50% by 2010. This is the most notable growth among the four materials. Lastly, plastics had the lowest recycling rates, with an initial figure close to negligible in 1982. However, the recycling rate for plastics showed a steady increase over the years, reaching just around 10% by 2010.

Comparing among the materials, it's clear that paper and cardboard recycling has always been prominent, though it experienced some fluctuations. Glass recycling showed moderate improvement, maintaining its position between paper and the other two materials. In contrast, the recycling rates of aluminum and plastics started much lower but demonstrated a consistent upward trend, with aluminum's growth being particularly steep. By the end of the period, aluminum cans had overtaken glass containers in terms of recycling rate growth. Despite its growth, plastic recycling remained considerably lower than the rates of the other three materials throughout the period observed.

This structured approach helps readers quickly grasp the essential information from the chart or graph, providing a concise yet comprehensive overview.

2. Using Descriptive Language to Convey Data Trends
1) Descriptive Language Cheat Sheet for Data Trends

The following terms are organized by the type of trend they are best used to describe to help students enrich their language when describing trends in data.

A. Increasing Trends

slight increase: a small or gradual rise.

moderate increase: a noticeable, yet not sharp rise.

sharp increase: a rapid and significant ascent.

skyrocketed: an extremely rapid increase; connotes surprise or unexpectedness.

surged: a powerful and often sudden upward movement.

B. Decreasing Trends

slight decrease: a small or gradual fall.

moderate decrease: a noticeable, yet not steep drop.

sharp decrease: a rapid and significant descent.

plummeted: a very steep and rapid drop; often used for dramatic decreases.

dipped: a temporary or slight drop.

C. Fluctuations

fluctuated: variations above and below a median point.

oscillated: moving back and forth in a regular pattern.

volatile: marked by rapid and unpredictable change.

saw-toothed: a pattern of sharp rises and falls.

D. Stability

remained steady: no change or very minor changes.

stabilized: returning to a steady state after variation.

plateaued: reaching a state of little or no change after a time of activity.

consistent: uniform; showing little variation.

E. Speed of Change

rapidly: occurring in a short time or at a fast pace.

gradually: taking place, or progressing, slowly over time.

abruptly: sudden or unexpected changes.

F. Extent of Change

marginal: very small changes that may be within the margin of error.

significant: enough to be noteworthy or of considerable amount.

dramatic: striking in extent or effect.

negligible: so small or unimportant as to be not worth considering.

G. Miscellaneous Descriptive Terms

peaked: reaching the highest point.

bottomed out: falling to the lowest point.

rebounded: recovered or bounced back after a decrease.

leveled off: when a rising or falling trend stops and one level is maintained.

H. Usage Examples

- In the first quarter, the stock price fluctuated wildly, but it stabilized by the end of the year.
- After the policy change, recycling rates skyrocketed, indicating a significant shift in consumer behavior.
- There was a marginal uptick in sales during the holiday season, followed by a moderate decrease.

This list can be used as a reference for your assignments involving data interpretation and description. Using a range of terms from this list will help you avoid repetition and make your data descriptions more vivid and precise.

2) Comparative Phrases and Structures in English

Comparative Phrases Handout

This handout is designed to enhance your ability to compare and contrast information effectively in English, especially when dealing with data and statistics. Utilizing these phrases and structures will enrich your analytical writing and discussions.

Basic Comparative Structures

more/less than/less than: used to compare quantities or degrees.

e.g., Sales in 2020 were more than sales in 2019.

as much as: used to denote equality in comparison.

e.g., The demand for renewable energy in 2020 was as much as in 2019.

higher/lower...than: for numerical or level comparisons.

e.g., The unemployment rate was higher in 2020 than in 2019.

Comparative Adjectives and Adverbs

-er / more...than: used with adjectives and adverbs to compare differences.

e.g., This year's profits are higher / more substantial than last year's.

the + comparative adjective, the + comparative adjective: to show that two changes happen together.

e.g., The more we invest in technology, the higher our efficiency climbs.

Phrases for Direct Comparisons

compared with: used to draw a direct comparison between two entities.

e.g., Compared with 2019, the 2020 sales figures show a significant increase.

in contrast to/with: to highlight differences.

e.g., In contrast to the declining oil sector, the renewable energy sector saw growth.

unlike: highlighting a stark difference.

e.g., Unlike last quarter, this quarter's performance has improved.

similarly: denoting similarity.

e.g., Similarly, both sectors have faced challenges this year.

as opposed to: used to contrast two options.

e.g., As opposed to cutting costs, the company focused on increasing revenue.

Phrases for Subtle Comparisons

whereas/while: introducing a contrast within the same sentence.

e.g., Whereas sales in Europe increased, those in Asia decreased.

both...and...: to compare two items that share a common feature.

e.g., Both the technology and healthcare sectors experienced growth.

neither...nor...: to show that two items share a lack of a feature.

e.g., Neither the marketing nor the sales department met their quarterly targets.

not only...but also...: to add information in a comparison.

e.g., The product was not only the most sold item but also the highest-rated by customers.

Phrases for Enhancing Comparisons

far more/less...than: emphasizing a significant difference.

e.g., The software sector is far more profitable than the hardware sector.

slightly/marginally/substantially: modifying the degree of comparison.

e.g., The costs were slightly lower this year than last year.

on par with: indicating equivalence.

e.g., The current inflation rate is on par with the central bank's target.

Example Sentences for Practice

- Compared with the last decade, the growth rate of urban populations has increased significantly.
- The GDP of Country A is far higher than that of Country B, whereas the unemployment rate is considerably lower.
- Both renewable energy consumption and electric vehicle sales have seen a substantial increase in the past year.
- Unlike in the previous year, this year's data shows a marginal increase in consumer spending.

- The company not only expanded its market share, but also improved its overall customer satisfaction ratings.

This handout should serve as a quick reference to improve the precision and clarity of your comparative analyses, enriching your academic and professional writing.

3. Synthesizing and Presenting Data

With the structure and language above, now the data can be clearly synthesized and presented. For example, the chart on Page 78 describes the recycling rate for the selected materials: 1982–2010.

It can be integrated with the following text.

The chart provides data on the recycling rates of four materials—paper and cardboard, glass containers, aluminum cans, and plastics—over a 28-year period from 1982 to 2010 in a specific country.

From a broad perspective, all four materials have shown an overall increase in their recycling rates over the observed period. Paper and cardboard started and remained as the most recycled material, with rates fluctuating between 65% and 80%. After a slight decline in the initial years, the recycling rate for this material steadied and maintained a position above 70% from 1986 onwards.

Glass container recycling showed modest growth, starting at around 50% in 1982 and ending at just above 60% by 2010. The trend for glass displays a slow but steady increase with minor fluctuations throughout the years.

Aluminum cans experienced the most significant growth. The recycling rate for this material started at just above 5% in 1982 and saw a nearly linear increase, finishing at approximately 45% in 2010. This sharp rise indicates a robust improvement in the recycling of aluminum cans over nearly three decades.

Plastics had the lowest recycling rate but showed the most growth percentage-wise. Starting at under 4% in 1982, the recycling rate for plastics rose steadily, ending at around 10% by 2010. Despite this increase, plastics remained the least recycled material of the four.

The overall comparison shows that while recycling rates have improved for all materials, the improvement was not uniform. Paper and cardboard and aluminum cans had notably higher recycling percentages, indicating possibly more established or efficient recycling processes or greater market demand for these recycled materials. In contrast, glass containers showed modest improvement, and plastics, despite doubling their recycling rate, lagged behind the other materials.

Class Activity 8: *Write a report to describe the following line graph.*

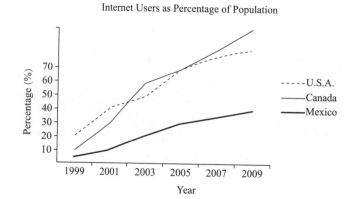

Class Activity 9: *Write a report to describe the following pie graphs.*

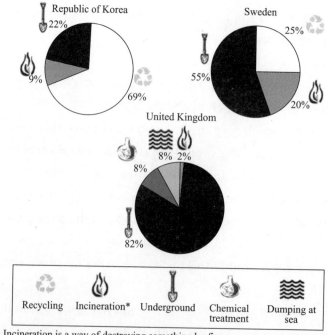

* Incineration is a way of destroying something by fire.

Class Activity 10: *Write a report to describe the following bar chart.*

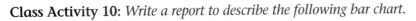

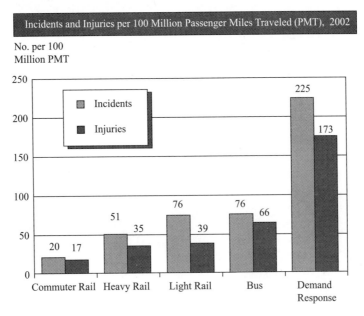

Incidents and Injuries per 100 Million Passenger Miles Traveled (PMT), 2002

No. per 100
Million PMT

Incidents

Injuries

Commuter Rail: 20, 17
Heavy Rail: 51, 35
Light Rail: 76, 39
Bus: 76, 66
Demand Response: 225, 173

Class Activity 11: *Write a report to describe the following flow chart.*

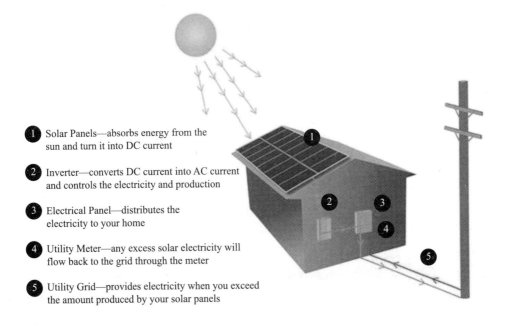

1 Solar Panels—absorbs energy from the sun and turn it into DC current

2 Inverter—converts DC current into AC current and controls the electricity and production

3 Electrical Panel—distributes the electricity to your home

4 Utility Meter—any excess solar electricity will flow back to the grid through the meter

5 Utility Grid—provides electricity when you exceed the amount produced by your solar panels

Class Activity 12: *Write a report to describe the following map.*

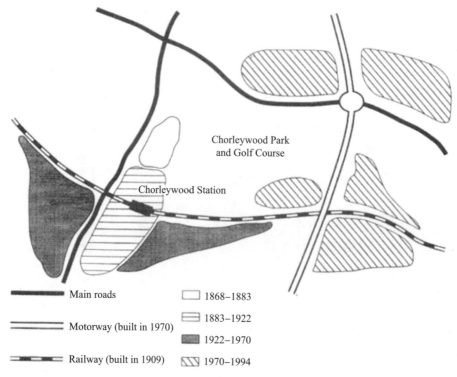

Village of Chorleywood Showing Development Between 1868 and 1994

4.4
Using Bullet Points and Lists

Bullet points are typographical marks or symbols that introduce items in a list. Usually, a bullet point is represented by a centered dot (•), but there are different forms of bullet points to pick from based on the writer's preference.

For example, diamond (◆), diamond cluster (∴), arrow (➤), and square (■) are other popular bullet point types that can be used. These can also be used to create a sub-bullet or nested bullet point following an initial bulleted idea. The important thing is to be consistent when using a different type of bullet points and not to mix them up, which negates their entire purpose.

4.4.1 Reasons for Using Bullet Points and Lists

Bullet points and lists are essential tools in both written and oral communication, offering a structured way to present information clearly and concisely. Their utility spans various contexts, from academic writing and business reports to presentations and online content. This section explores the reasons for using bullet points and lists and how they can enhance your communication.

1. **Clarity and Readability**

Simplification: Bullet points break down complex information into manageable, easily digestible pieces. This simplification helps the readers understand and retain information more effectively.

Organization: Lists organize information in a logical sequence, making it easier for the readers to follow the argument or narrative.

Highlighting Key Points: Bullet points draw attention to the most important aspects of your message, ensuring that key information is not overlooked.

For example:

> To make this recipe, you will need the following:
> - milk;
> - eggs;
> - butter;
> - sugar.

2. **Engagement and Retention**

Engagement: Bullet points and lists create a visual break in the text, making content more appealing and easier to engage with, especially in long documents or articles.

Retention: Information presented in bullet points or lists is easier to remember. The structure facilitates recall by creating a mental "map" of the information.

For example:

> In order to be successful, you want to consider the following steps to ensure financial stability:
> - Pay off all debts;
> - Keep three months' worth of bill payments in savings;

- Invest a percentage of your check each month.

3. Efficiency and Effectiveness

Time-saving: For both the writer and the reader, bullet points convey essential information quickly, without the need for lengthy paragraphs. This efficiency is particularly valuable in an era where time is precious, and attention spans are short.

Versatility: Bullet points and lists are versatile and can be used in various contexts to enhance clarity, whether in reports, e-mails, presentations, or online content.

Comparison and Contrast: Lists are an effective way to present comparisons or contrasts between different items, ideas, or data points, making differences and similarities clear at a glance.

For example:

> To finish glazing the cake, follow these steps:
> - Mix the sugar, flavoring, and water in a bowl;
> - Remove the cake from the oven;
> - Immediately pour 3/4 of the glaze over the hot cake;
> - Allow the cake to cool;
> - Drizzle the remaining glaze over the top.

4. Enhancing Persuasiveness

Emphasis on Benefits or Features: In marketing materials or business proposals, bullet points can effectively highlight product benefits or project features, making a persuasive case to the readers.

Actionable Items: Lists can clearly outline steps or actions that need to be taken, making it easier for the readers to understand what is required and act accordingly.

For example:

> To wrap it up, studying before an exam is much better than cramming the night before. To make this effective, you should do the following:
> - Gather all your study materials, notes, and text one week in advance;
> - Organize these materials by level of difficulty;
> - Spend 15 to 20 minutes each night reviewing these materials;
> - Review all main points the night before the exam.

5. Visual Appeal

Bullet points and lists add to the aesthetic appeal of the text, creating a visually organized layout that is pleasing to the eye and encourages the readers to continue engaging with the content.

The use of bullet points and lists is a powerful strategy to enhance the effectiveness of your communication. By offering clarity, improving readability, and ensuring information is memorable, they serve as crucial elements in making your message impactful. Whether you're writing an academic paper, delivering a business report, or crafting a marketing message, incorporating bullet points and lists can significantly contribute to the success of your communication efforts.

Class Activity 13: *Convert the following paragraph into an easy-to-read list using bullet points and work in groups to discuss the effectiveness of the conversion in class.*

Acme Corp is a leading provider of business solutions, offering a wide range of services designed to enhance productivity and efficiency for organizations of all sizes. Our flagship product, Acme Workspace, is a comprehensive suite of tools for project management, including real-time collaboration features, task tracking, and customizable report generation. In addition to Acme Workspace, we offer Acme Secure, a state-of-the-art cybersecurity service that protects against data breaches with advanced encryption, continuous monitoring, and immediate incident response. Our professional services team is adept at implementing bespoke software solutions tailored to the unique needs of each client, ensuring seamless integration with existing systems. Acme Corp also provides ongoing support and training services to help clients maximize the use of our products and maintain optimal performance.

4.4.2 Crafting Effective Bullet Points

Creating effective bullet points is an art that enhances readability, clarity, and engagement in written communication. Whether you're drafting a report, making a presentation slide, or preparing content for digital media, well-crafted bullet points can significantly improve the delivery of your message. This section provides guidelines on how to create impactful bullet points that effectively convey your information.

1. Starting with a Strong Lead-In

Ensure your bullet points are introduced by a consistent lead-in sentence or phrase. This sets the stage for your list and prepares the information that follows for the readers.

Here's an example illustrating how to effectively introduce bullet points with a strong lead-in.

Context: Imagine you're writing a section in a business proposal about the benefits of a new project management software your company is offering.

Our new project management software, ProjectPro Plus, is designed to streamline team collaboration and enhance productivity. Key benefits include:

> Strong Lead-In

> Bullet Points Following the Lead-In

- **Effortless Task Management:** Assign, track, and manage tasks with a few clicks, ensuring projects stay on schedule.
- **Real-time Communication Tools:** Integrated chat and video conferencing features facilitate instant communication among team members, regardless of their location.
- **Comprehensive Reporting:** Generate detailed reports in seconds to monitor project progress and team performance.
- **Customizable Dashboards:** Personalize your workspace with widgets and metrics relevant to your project needs.
- **Enhanced Security Measures:** State-of-the-art encryption and data protection protocols keep your project information safe and secure.

The lead-in sentence clearly sets the stage for the bullet points by stating the purpose of the software and what the readers can expect to learn from the following list. It's concise yet informative, which directly leads into the detailed benefits outlined in the bullet points. This approach helps maintain focus and ensures the readers understand the context before diving into the specifics.

2. Keeping It Concise

Keeping bullet points concise is essential for clarity and effectiveness. Here're some examples demonstrating how to make bullet points succinct, focusing on delivering key information directly and efficiently.

Original Examples	Concise Examples
Provides users with the ability to quickly and easily assign tasks to team members, which enhances the overall workflow efficiency.	Enables quick task assignment, boosting workflow efficiency.
Offers an integrated communication platform that includes features like instant messaging and video conferencing, allowing team members to collaborate in real-time.	Includes instant messaging and video conferencing for real-time collaboration.
The software is capable of generating comprehensive reports that allow project managers to keep track of project progress and monitor the performance of the team members effectively.	Generates detailed reports for tracking project progress and team performance.
Users have the option to customize their dashboards in such a way that they can include widgets and metrics that are most relevant to their specific project needs and requirements.	Allows dashboard customization with relevant widgets and metrics.
Our project management tool is equipped with state-of-the-art encryption and data protection protocols designed to ensure that all of your project information remains safe and secure from unauthorized access.	Features top-notch encryption and data protection to secure project information.

Conciseness in bullet points improves readability and ensures that the readers can quickly grasp the essential information without wading through unnecessary details. This approach respects readers' time and attention, making your communication more effective.

Brevity Is Key: Each bullet point should be a concise statement. The aim is to have a clear and direct presentation of information without unnecessary words.

Focus on Essentials: Each bullet point should include only the most relevant information as bullet points are not the place for detailed explanations but rather for key facts, ideas, or actions.

3. **Maintaining a Parallel Structure**

Maintaining a parallel structure in bullet points involves using the same grammatical form within each point to create a consistent and balanced list. This approach enhances readability and coherence. Here're some examples demonstrating how to maintain a parallel structure in bullet points.

Without Parallel Structure	With Parallel Structure
Features of a Product	
Easy to use	• Easy to use
Fast processing speed	• Fast processing speed
The design is sleek	• Sleek design
Instructions for a Process	
Fill out the application form	• Fill out the application form
Submit your documents	• Submit your documents
Wait for a confirmation e-mail	• Wait for a confirmation e-mail
Benefits of a Service	
24/7 customer support	• 24/7 customer support
You can save money	• Money-saving opportunities
Reduction of time spent on tasks	• Reduced time spent on tasks
Job Responsibilities	
Managing a team	• Managing a team
To develop marketing strategies	• Developing marketing strategies
Creation of reports	• Creating reports

Maintaining a parallel structure in bullet points not only makes the content more professional and easier to read but also ensures that the information is presented in a logically consistent manner. This technique is crucial for effective written communication, particularly in contexts requiring clarity and precision, such as academic writing, business reports, and instructional materials.

4. Using Bullet Points for the Right Purpose

Using bullet points effectively means choosing the right contexts and purposes where they can enhance clarity, organization, and reader engagement. Here're some examples illustrating how to use bullet points appropriately to convey the information effectively.

Example 1: Outlining Features of a Product

Purpose: to concisely list the key features of a new smartphone model.

- High-resolution camera with night mode
- Water-and dust-resistant design
- All-day battery life
- 5G connectivity for faster Internet speeds
- Edge-to-edge OLED display

In this example, bullet points effectively highlight the distinct features of the product, making it easy for readers to scan and understand the selling points at a glance.

Example 2: Providing Instructions or Steps

- Purpose: to clearly outline the steps required to install a software application.
- Download the installer from the official website.
- Open the downloaded file to start the installation process.
- Follow the on-screen instructions to customize your installation.
- Accept the license agreement to proceed.
- Click "Finish" to complete the installation.

Using bullet points breaks down the whole process into simple, actionable steps, making it easier for users to follow and execute the instructions.

Example 3: Listing Benefits or Advantages

Purpose: to succinctly present the benefits of subscribing to a digital news service.

- Unlimited access to articles and reports
- Exclusive content not available to non-subscribers
- Weekly newsletters with insights and analysis

- Discounts on events and conferences
- Support for ad-free browsing

Bullet points efficiently communicate the value proposition of the subscription service, enabling potential subscribers to quickly assess the benefits.

Example 4: Summarizing Research Findings or Data Points

Purpose: to summarize the key findings from a market research report.

- 75% of consumers prefer online shopping to in-store purchases.
- Smartphone apps account for 60% of all e-commerce transactions.
- Free shipping is the most significant factor influencing purchase decisions.
- Customer reviews impact the buying choices of 85% of respondents.

Bullet points distill complex research findings into accessible, memorable data points, facilitating quick comprehension and retention of the information.

Example 5: Highlighting Agenda Items or Meeting Points

Purpose: to outline the agenda for a team meeting.

- Review of last week's project milestones
- Discussion on client feedback and revisions
- Planning for the upcoming sprint
- Team availability and resource allocation
- Any other business (AOB)

Using bullet points to list agenda items organizes the meeting structure, ensuring that all topics are addressed systematically and efficiently.

Bullet points are a versatile tool for enhancing written communication across various contexts. When used for the right purposes, such as listing features, providing instructions, summarizing benefits or findings, and organizing agendas or meeting points, they make the information more accessible, engaging, and actionable for the readers.

5. Ensuring Clarity and Impact

Ensuring clarity and impact with bullet points means crafting each point to be straightforward and meaningful, directly conveying value or critical information to the readers. Here're some examples demonstrating how to achieve clarity and impact in bullet points across different contexts.

Less Clear and Impactful	More Clear and Impactful
Example 1: Product Description	
Our product comes in various colors and sizes, suitable for a wide range of customers depending on their preferences and needs, which can vary widely.	Available in multiple colors and sizes to suit every preference.
Example 2: Service Benefits	
By subscribing to our service, customers might potentially see an improvement in their overall efficiency, which could lead to better outcomes over time.	Boost efficiency immediately, ensuring improved outcomes.
Example 3: Instructions for Use	
Users should consider starting the machine by pressing the big button on the front after ensuring it's plugged in and ready to go for the best experience.	Press the power button to start—ensure the device is plugged in.
Example 4: Resumé Skills Section	
I have a good amount of experience working with teams on various projects, which has allowed me to develop strong collaborative skills over time.	Experienced in team collabora-tion on diverse projects.
Example 5: Event Highlights	
The event will feature a number of interesting activities, including talks from industry leaders, workshops on various topics, and networking opportunities that attendees will find beneficial.	Keynotes from industry leaders, interactive workshops, and networking sessions.

Achieving clarity and impact in bullet points involves using concise language, focusing on the essence of the message, and avoiding unnecessary details. This approach ensures that the readers can quickly understand and appreciate the significance of the information presented, making your communication more effective and engaging.

6. Limiting the Number of Bullet Points

Optimal Number: Avoid overwhelming the readers by limiting the number of bullet points. A good rule of thumb is to aim for 3 to 7 points, depending on the context and depth of the information being presented.

Limiting the number of bullet points is crucial to maintain the readers' attention and ensure the information is memorable and impactful. Overloading with too many points can dilute the message and overwhelm the readers. Here're some examples illustrating the effective limitation of bullet points.

Too Many Bullet Points	Limited and Focused Bullet Points
Example 1: Product Features	
• High-resolution camera	• High-resolution camera with night mode
• Water-resistant up to 30 meters	• Water-resistant and 24-hour battery life
• 24-hour battery life	• 5G connectivity and wireless charging
• Wireless charging capability	• Biometric security with dual SIM support
• OLED display	
• 5G connectivity	
• Biometric security	
• Dual SIM support	
• Expandable storage up to 1TB	
• Noise cancellation audio	
• Environmentally friendly materials	
• Customizable exterior	
Example 2: Service Benefits	
• 24/7 customer support	• 24/7 customer support and money-back guarantee
• Money-back guarantee	• Free shipping and loyalty rewards program
• Free shipping on all orders	• Access to exclusive sales and customization services
• Loyalty rewards program	
• Access to exclusive sales	
• Gift wrapping options	

- Easy returns and exchanges
- Personal shopping assistant
- Customization services
- Sustainable packaging

- Sustainable packaging and easy returns

Example 3: Resumé Skills

- Project management
- Team leadership
- Budgeting and finance
- Data analysis
- Strategic planning
- Public speaking
- Digital marketing
- SEO expertise
- Social media management
- Content creation
- Graphic design
- Software proficiency

- Project management and team leadership
- Budgeting, finance, and strategic planning
- Digital marketing, including SEO and social media
- Content creation and graphic design skills

Limiting the number of bullet points to present information in a focused, concise manner helps ensure that readers can easily engage with and remember the content. This approach is especially beneficial in contexts where you want to highlight the most critical points without overwhelming or losing readers' attention.

7. Ending with a Strong Conclusion or Call to Action

Ending bullet points with a strong conclusion or call to action (CTA) is crucial for guiding readers towards a desired outcome or next step. This technique solidifies the message's impact and encourages engagement. Here're some examples across different contexts to illustrate this approach.

Bullet Points	Strong Conclusion / CTA
Example 1: Product Feature List	
• High-resolution camera with night mode for stunning photos • Water-resistant up to 30 meters, ensuring durability in all conditions • 24-hour battery life to keep you connected longer • 5G connectivity for ultra-fast Internet speeds	Experience the future of smartphones today. Order your XPhone now and elevate your tech game!
Example 2: Service Benefits	
• 24/7 customer support to assist you anytime • Flexible pricing plans tailored to your needs • Customizable services to match your unique requirements • State-of-the-art security measures to protect your data	Don't let these opportunities pass you by. Sign up today to take your business to the next level with our tailored solutions.
Example 3: Health Program Advantages	
• Personalized diet plans based on your health goals • Weekly check-ins with a certified nutritionist • Access to a supportive online community • Exclusive workout routines designed by fitness experts	Join our wellness journey now and transform your life. Your healthier future starts today!
Example 4: Workshop Announcement	
• Interactive sessions with industry-leading experts • Hands-on projects to apply your new skills • Networking opportunities with professionals in your field • Certificate of completion to add to your portfolio	Secure your spot now! Elevate your career with our expert-led workshop. Spaces are limited.

Example 5: Environmental Campaign

- Reduce plastic use to save marine life
- Adopt renewable energy to combat climate change
- Support sustainable agriculture to protect biodiversity
- Volunteer for local clean-up efforts to enhance community spaces

Take action for the planet today. Join our movement and make a real

difference. Every action counts!

A strong conclusion or call to action effectively wraps up the message delivered through bullet points, providing readers with a clear direction or next steps. Whether encouraging a purchase, sign-up, participation, or lifestyle change, a well-crafted CTA can significantly increase engagement and achieve desired outcomes.

Unit 5
Business Vocabulary and Expressions

Effective business writing goes beyond grammar and punctuation; it hinges on the precise choice of words and expressions. The vocabulary and expressions you use can shape how your message is perceived, convey professionalism, and establish a strong connection with your audience. This section delves into the art of selecting the right words and crafting impactful expressions for various business situations.

5.1
Business Vocabulary

In the realm of business English, having a robust vocabulary is akin to having a well-stocked toolbox. The words you choose to wield in your communication can greatly influence the impression you leave on your peers, clients, and superiors. This section delves into the essential business vocabulary you need to navigate the intricacies of the corporate world.

Class Activity 1: *Finish the following pre-assessment quiz before you begin.*

Instructions: Please answer the following questions to the best of your ability. This quiz is designed to assess your current understanding of business vocabulary. There are no right or wrong answers. Your responses will help us tailor the course content to your needs.

Section 1: Vocabulary Categories

1. Which term is used to describe the financial record of a company's revenue, expenses, and profits over a specific period?

    A) Analysis
    B) Income statement
    C) Audit
    D) Investment

2. In the business context, what does the acronym "CEO" stand for?

    A) Chief Executive Officer.

    B) Chief Experience Officer.

    C) Customer Engagement Officer.

    D) Certified Executive Organizer.

Section 2: Word Origins and Meanings

3. From which language does the term "entrepreneur" originate?

    A) Latin
    B) Greek
    C) French
    D) German

4. What does the term "merger" refer to in business?

    A) A business expanding its product line.

    B) A company being acquired by another.

    C) A partnership between two small businesses.

    D) The process of outsourcing.

Section 3: Vocabulary Expansion Strategies

5. Which of the following is not a recommended strategy for expanding your business vocabulary?

    A) Reading business-related books and articles.

    B) Engaging in professional networking events.

    C) Avoiding any exposure to unfamiliar terms.

    D) Watching industry-related webinars and seminars.

6. Which term describes the study of how consumers make decisions and how businesses can understand and influence those decisions?

    A) Economics
    B) Management
    C) Marketing
    D) Sociology

Section 4: Industry-specific Vocabulary

7. In the tech industry, what does "AI" stand for?

    A) Artificial Intelligence.
    B) Advanced Interface.
    C) Automated Information.
    D) Applicable Infrastructure.

8. Which term refers to the funds that a company raises by selling ownership shares in the company?

A) Loan　　　　B) Revenue　　　　C) Equity　　　D) Asset

Section 5: Simulated Business Scenarios

9. You need to write a formal letter to request sponsorship for an upcoming charity event. Which tone would be the most appropriate for this communication?

   A) Casual and informal .　　　　　B) Professional and formal.

   C) Humorous and light-hearted.　　D) Critical and confrontational.

10. You are composing an e-mail to inform your team about changes in the project timeline. Which subject line effectively communicates this message?

   A) "Important News!"　　　　　B) "Meeting Next Week"

   C) "Project Timeline Update"　　D) "Team Gathering"

Note: This quiz is designed to gauge learners' existing knowledge of business vocabulary. It covers various aspects of business terminology, from general concepts to industry-specific terms. The quiz provides insight into learners' familiarity with different categories of business vocabulary and serves as a basis for tailoring the course content accordingly.

5.1.1 Categories of Business Vocabulary

Business vocabulary can be broadly categorized into several key areas, each serving a specific purpose in professional communication. Here are some of the most common categories:

1. Core Business Concepts

Understanding and employing fundamental business concepts enhances the credibility of your writing. Key terms include:

revenue: income generated from sales and services	收入：通过销售和服务产生的收入
profit: positive financial gain after deducting expenses	利润：扣除费用后的正向财务收益
market share: portion of the total market that a company holds	市场份额：公司在总市场中所占的部分

ROI (Return on Investment): measurement of profitability relative to the initial investment	**投资回报率**：相对于初始投资的营利性度量
synergy: interaction that enhances the combined effect of different elements	**协同效应**：不同元素互动增强的联合效果

2. Communication and Collaboration

Effective communication and collaboration rely on precise language. Key terms include:

synchronize: coordinating activities to ensure alignment	**同步**：协调活动以确保一致性
engage: interacting and involving stakeholders in meaningful discussions	**参与**：与利益相关者进行有意义的互动和交流
collaborate: working together to achieve a common goal	**协作**：共同努力实现共同目标
convey: expressing or communicating information clearly	**表达**：清晰地传达或交流信息
alignment: ensuring consistency and agreement among team members	**一致性**：确保团队成员间的一致性和协调

3. Strategy and Planning

Describing strategic concepts demonstrates your grasp of organizational planning. Key terms include:

strategy: long-term approach designed to achieve specific goals	**战略**：旨在实现特定目标的长期方法
tactics: specific actions taken to execute a strategy	**策略**：执行战略所采取的具体行动
benchmark: standard used for comparison to measure performance	**基准**：用于比较以测量绩效的标准

milestone: significant achievement or point of progress	里程碑：重大成就或进展点
initiative: action plan or project designed to achieve a goal	倡议：旨在实现目标的行动计划或项目

4. Leadership and Management

Conveying effective leadership requires the use of pertinent vocabulary. Key terms include:

delegate: entrusting tasks or responsibilities to others	委派：将任务或责任委托给他人
empower: giving authority and autonomy to individuals or teams	授权：给予个人或团队权力和自主权
motivate: inspiring and encouraging individuals to take action	激励：鼓励个人采取行动
accountability: responsibility for actions and outcomes	责任：对行动和结果的责任
mentor: guiding and providing support to less experienced individuals	导师：指导并为经验较少的个人提供支持

5. Financial Terminology

Precision in financial discussions relies on accurate financial vocabulary. Key terms include:

assets: resources owned by a company or individual	资产：公司或个人拥有的资源
liabilities: debts or obligations owed by a company	负债：公司所欠的债务或义务
cash flow: movement of money in and out of a business	现金流：企业的资金进出
balance sheet: financial statement showing assets, liabilities, and equity	资产负债表：显示资产、负债和所有者权益的财务报表

forecast: predicted financial projection for a specific period

预测：特定时期的预测财务展望

6. Customer Relations

Effective customer-centric communication calls for specific customer-oriented terms. Key terms include:

client: customer who engages in a professional relationship	**客户：**在专业关系中从事业务的顾客
customer satisfaction: a measure of how well products or services meet customer expectations	**客户满意度：**衡量产品或服务满足客户期望的程度
feedback: input or responses from customers on products or services	**反馈：**客户对产品或服务的输入或响应
retention: keeping customers engaged and loyal over time	**保留：**长期保持客户的参与和忠诚
value proposition: unique benefits that a product or service offers to customers	**价值主张：**产品或服务提供给客户的独特好处

7. Marketing Vocabulary

Marketing involves promoting and selling products or services to customers. Key terms include:

target audience: the specific group of people a product or service is aimed at	**目标受众：**产品或服务针对的特定人群
brand awareness: the extent to which customers recognize and remember a brand	**品牌意识：**客户识别和记住品牌的程度
market research: gathering and analyzing data about customer preferences and market trends	**市场研究：**收集和分析有关客户偏好和市场趋势的数据

market segmentation: the process of dividing a broad target market into smaller, more manageable segments based on common characteristics	**市场细分**：根据共同特征将广泛的目标市场划分为更小、更易管理的细分市场的过程
brand equity: the perceived value and strength of a brand in the market	**品牌资产**：市场中品牌的知名度和价值

8. Finance Vocabulary

Finance deals with managing money, investments, and financial transactions. Key terms include:

profit margin: the difference between revenue and costs, expressed as a percentage	**利润率**：收入和成本之间的差异，用百分比表示
budget: a financial plan detailing income, expenses, and allocations	**预算**：详细说明收入、支出和分配的财务计划
budget allocation: the process of distributing a budget to various expenses and activities	**预算分配**：将预算分配给各种费用和活动的过程

9. Human Resources (HR) Vocabulary

HR focuses on managing employees and their needs within an organization. Key terms include:

onboarding: the process of integrating new employees into the organization	**入职**：将新员工融入组织的过程
performance appraisal: the evaluation of an employee's work performance	**绩效评估**：评价员工工作绩效的过程
diversity and inclusion: efforts to create a workplace that values differences and promotes equality	**多样性与包容性**：努力创建一个尊重差异和促进平等的工作环境
termination: the formal ending of an employee's employment with a company	**终止**：正式结束员工与公司的雇佣关系

10. Operations Vocabulary

Operations pertain to the day-to-day activities that keep a business running. Key terms include:

logistics: managing the movement of goods, services, and information	物流：管理货物、服务和信息的流动
efficiency: achieving maximum output with minimal input	效率：用最少的投入实现最大的产出
supply chain: the network of organizations involved in producing and distributing products	供应链：参与生产和分销产品的组织网络

11. Sales Vocabulary

Sales involve convincing customers to purchase products or services. Key terms include:

lead generation: identifying potential customers or clients	潜在客户生成：识别潜在顾客或客户
closing the deal: finalizing a sale and securing the purchase	完成交易：最终确定销售并确保购买
upselling: encouraging customers to buy more expensive or additional products	升级销售：鼓励客户购买更昂贵或额外的产品

By familiarizing yourself with the specialized vocabulary within each category, you can navigate the diverse aspects of business with clarity and precision.

Class Activity 2: *Fill in the following gaps with the correct words or expressions related to business.*

1. In today's highly _____ business environment, companies must adapt quickly to market changes.

2. Our new marketing strategy aims to _____ brand awareness and attract a larger customer base.

3. The team's ability to work _____ and efficiently is crucial to meeting project deadlines.

4. Effective _____ management is essential to keep our projects within budget.

5. To improve customer satisfaction, we should _____ our customer support services.

6. The company's recent expansion into international markets has brought about several _____ challenges.

7. We need to _____ our inventory levels to ensure we can meet customer demand.

8. Please prepare a detailed _____ of the quarterly sales figures for the board meeting.

9. The CEO's _____ leadership style has motivated employees to perform at their best.

10. We should consider implementing cost-cutting _____ to improve our financial performance.

11. The team's _____ in the negotiation led to a successful partnership agreement.

12. Developing a strong online presence is a key _____ in today's digital age.

13. The company's commitment to _____ responsibility is reflected in its sustainable practices.

14. Effective _____ communication is crucial when addressing customer complaints.

15. We must _____ our resources wisely to maximize efficiency and profitability.

5.1.2 Origins of Business Terms

Have you ever wondered where the terms and phrases commonly used in the business world originate? Understanding the origins of business vocabulary can provide valuable insights into their meanings and usage. Many business terms have fascinating historical backgrounds, and knowing their roots can enhance your grasp of these expressions.

1. Latin and Greek Roots
Many business terms find their origins in Latin and Greek. These classical

languages have contributed numerous words and phrases, particularly in fields like law, finance, and science. For example:

- "Ad hoc" (Latin) means "for this purpose". In business, it's often used to describe solutions or arrangements created specifically for a particular situation.
- "Eureka" (Greek) translates to "I have found it". It's famously attributed to Archimedes and is used to express the joy of discovering a solution or breakthrough.
- "Bene" (Latin) means "good". It's often used to denote a positive outcome or advantage.
- "Chronos" (Greek) means "time". It's often used to refer to events arranged in order of occurrence.

2. Old English and Germanic Influence

English itself has deep Germanic roots, and this influence is evident in many everyday business terms. For example:

- "Trade" (Old English "trædu") has a long history in commerce and refers to the buying and selling of goods and services.
- "Deal" (Old English "dælan") originally meant "to distribute", which is still a core aspect of many business transactions.

3. French Influence

French has left a substantial imprint on the English language, particularly in areas like diplomacy, law, and finance. For example:

- "Entrepreneur" comes from the French word "entreprendre", which means "to undertake". It refers to someone who takes on the risk and responsibility of starting a new business.
- "Finance" has French origin in "financer", which means "to provide funds". It's a central term in the world of business and economics.

4. Industrial Revolution Influence

Terms related to industry and manufacturing emerged during the Industrial

Revolution. For example:

- "Assembly line" means a production process where products move along a line, with each worker specializing in a specific task.
- "Mass production" means the large-scale manufacturing of standardized products, made possible by efficient machinery.
- "Automation" means the use of machines or technology to perform tasks without human intervention.
- "Factory" means a facility equipped for large-scale manufacturing, a hallmark of the Industrial Revolution.
- "Textile" means a type of woven fabric, and textiles were a prominent industry during the Industrial Revolution.
- "Urbanization" means the process of population shift from rural to urban areas due to industrial growth.

5. Cultural Adaptations

Business terms often adapt to cultural contexts. For example:

- "Fengshui" is a Chinese term for harmonizing environments, used metaphorically for business organizations.
- "Kaizen" is a Japanese term meaning continuous improvement, widely used in business management.
- "Guanxi" is a Chinese term for building and nurturing relationships, crucial in business contexts.
- "Maktub" is an Arabic word meaning "it is written", often used to express acceptance of fate in business decisions.
- "Gemütlichkeit" is a German term describing a sense of comfort and coziness, important for fostering positive workplace environments.
- "Dharma" is a concept from Hinduism, often adapted to business contexts to reflect ethical and moral responsibilities.
- "Punctuality" means the value of being on time, which varies across cultures, influencing business interactions.
- "Jugaad" is an Indian term for innovative and resourceful problem-solving, applicable to entrepreneurial endeavors.

6. **Decoding Unfamiliar Terms**

Understanding word roots can be a valuable strategy for deciphering the meanings of unfamiliar business terms. For example:

- telecommunication: "Tele" (from Greek "tele") means "far" or "distant", and "communication" refers to sharing information. Together, "tele-communication" refers to the distant exchange of information.
- interpersonal: "Inter" (from Latin "inter") means "between" or "among", and "personal" relates to individuals. Thus, "interpersonal" signifies interactions between people.

Understanding these linguistic origins can help you decipher the meanings of unfamiliar business terms. It's a testament to the rich tapestry of language and the way it evolves to suit the needs of different fields and eras. As you explore the world of business vocabulary, keep in mind the historical journey that has shaped these expressions into what they are today.

Class Activity 3: *Explore the origins of the following business terms and deduce their meanings.*

1. ad hoc
2. ad infinitum
3. de facto
4. in loco parentis
5. per diem
6. democracy
7. economics
8. telecommunication
9. autonomy
10. metropolis
11. chronology

Class Activity 4: *Finish the following business vocabulary post-assessment quiz.*

Instructions: Answer all the questions to the best of your ability. Choose the most appropriate answer to each question. This quiz consists of multiple-choice questions and definition matching.

Section 1: Multiple Choices

1. Which term refers to the large-scale manufacturing of standardized products?
   A) Customization
   B) Automation
   C) Mass production
   D) Specialization

2. Which term describes a system where people have the authority to make decisions?

   A) Hierarchy   B) Bureaucracy   C) Democracy   D) Monarchy

3. Which culture does the term "Kaizen" originate from?

   A) Chinese   B) Indian   C) Japanese   D) Russian

Section 2: Definition Matching

Guanxi   A) A system of government where a monarch rules

Punctuality   B) A Chinese term for building and nurturing relationships

Monarchy   C) A German term describing a sense of comfort and coziness

Gemütlicheit   D) The value of being on time, varying across cultures

Section 3: Blank Filling

1. A written agreement between two parties detailing the terms of a business transaction is called a(n) _____.

2. The process of producing goods on a large scale using efficient machinery is known as _____.

Section 4: True or False

1. Code of conduct is a comprehensive handbook that outlines company policies. (   )

2. Interpersonal signifies interactions between individuals. (   )

Section 5: Word Scrambling (Unscramble the Term)

LNNMAENAMTCE

5.2
Idiomatic Expressions

Idiomatic expressions, often referred to as idioms, are phrases or combinations of words with meanings that cannot be deduced from the literal definitions of the individual words. These expressions have cultural, historical, or figurative significance and are commonly used in both spoken and written language. In the context of business writing, mastering idiomatic expressions can significantly enhance your communication skills. This section explores the importance of idioms, different types of business idioms, and how to use them effectively.

Class Activity 5: *Guess the meanings of the following idiomatic expressions and then provide an example sentence for each.*

1. **put your best foot forward**

   Meaning:

   Example:

2. **read between the lines**

   Meaning:

   Example:

3. **ballpark figure**

   Meaning:

   Example:

4. **on the same page**

   Meaning:

   Example:

5. **think outside the box**

   Meaning:

   Example:

6. **turning point**

   Meaning:

   Example:

7. **bite off more than you can chew**

   Meaning:

   Example:

8. **get the ball rolling**

   Meaning:

   Example:

9. **raise the bar**

   Meaning:

   Example:

10. **behind the scenes**

Meaning:

Example:

5.2.1 Literal vs. Figurative Meanings of Idiomatic Expressions

If we take the idiom "hit the ground running" literally, it would mean physically hitting the ground while running. Of course, this doesn't make sense in the context of business communication.

In business and professional contexts, the figurative meaning of this idiom is to start a new task, project, or job quickly and effectively, without any delays or difficulties. It implies that someone is well-prepared and ready to make an immediate impact.

Imagine you're talking about a new employee who recently joined your team. You might say: "Our new marketing manager really hit the ground running. She came in with fresh ideas, formed strong connections, and contributed significantly to our recent campaign."

In this example, the figurative meaning of "hit the ground running" is used to emphasize the new employee's quick and impactful start in her role.

By understanding both the literal and figurative meanings of idiomatic expressions like this, you'll be able to use them appropriately and effectively in your business communication.

5.2.2 Cultural Nuances of Idiomatic Expressions

Idioms can be culturally nuanced, and their meanings might vary in different cultures. Here are a few examples illustrating how the same idiom can have different interpretations in various cultural contexts.

1. bite the bullet
- Western interpretation: to face a difficult situation bravely, even though it might be painful.
- Japanese interpretation: to make a difficult decision without delay.
2. break a leg
   Western interpretation: a way to wish someone good luck before a performance or presentation.

Turkish interpretation: an offensive term that could be interpreted negatively.

3. Cat's got your tongue?

Western interpretation: asking someone why they're not speaking or have suddenly become silent.

Arabic interpretation: accusing someone of lying or withholding information.

4. Curiosity killed the cat

Western interpretation: warning against being too nosy or asking too many questions.

Chinese interpretation: encouraging curiosity and inquisitiveness.

5. save face

Western interpretation: avoiding embarrassment or preserving one's reputation.

Chinese interpretation: maintaining honor and dignity, even in difficult situations.

6. piece of cake

Western interpretation: describing something as easy or simple.

Russian interpretation: referring to something that is not achievable or unrealistic.

It's crucial to recognize that idiomatic expressions might not be directly translated between languages and cultures. When communicating with individuals from diverse backgrounds, it's essential to be aware of these cultural differences to avoid misunderstandings. As you use idioms, consider the context and audience to ensure your message is received as intended.

5.2.3 Types of Business Idioms

Business idioms cover various aspects of the corporate world. Here are some common categories of business idiomatic expressions.

1. Financial Idioms

These idioms relate to money, finance, and economic situations. For example:

- in the red: operating at a financial loss
- cut corners: to save money by reducing costs
- make ends meet: to manage finances to cover expenses

2. Management Idioms

These idioms often describe leadership and decision-making. For example:

- call the shots: to make important decisions and having control
- beat the clock: to complete a task before a deadline
- on the back burner: postponing something for later

3. Sales and Marketing Idioms

These idioms are relevant to selling products and services. "Close the deal" is a well-known sales idiom, signifying successfully completing a sale.

4. Teamwork and Collaboration Idioms

Teamwork and collaboration idioms highlight the importance of cooperation, communication, and mutual effort in achieving shared goals. These expressions are commonly used to describe effective teamwork and group dynamics. For example:

- on the same page: having a shared understanding and alignment
- pull one's weight: to contribute actively and fairly to a team effort
- bargain in good faith: to negotiate honestly and sincerely
- give and take: to compromise and make concessions during negotiations
- get down to brass tacks: to discuss essential details and specifics
- keep someone in the loop: to keep someone informed about a situation
- read between the lines: to understand the hidden meaning in someone's words
- talk shop: to discuss work-related topics

5. Change and Innovation Idioms

These idioms describe adaptation and progress. For example:

- call the shots: to make important decisions and have control
- sit on the fence: to be undecided about something
- think outside the box: to find creative solutions beyond conventional thinking
- put out fires: to address urgent issues or crises

5.2.4 Using Idiomatic Expressions in Business Writing

To effectively incorporate idiomatic expressions into your business writing, consider the following tips.

- **Context Matters:** Ensure that the idiom you choose fits the context of your message. An idiom related to teamwork might not be suitable in a financial report.

- **Avoid Overuse:** Don't overload your writing with idioms. Use them sparingly to maintain clarity.

- **Know the Meaning:** Understand the precise meaning of the idiom and its connotations before using it.

- **Be Culturally Aware:** Be mindful of cultural differences. What's a common idiom in one culture might not have the same meaning in another.

- **Edit Carefully:** Review your writing to ensure that the idiom enhances your message without causing confusion.

- **Practice:** Like any aspect of writing, using idiomatic expressions effectively requires practice. Read widely and pay attention to how idioms are used in professional contexts.

Incorporating idiomatic expressions into your business writing can elevate your communication skills and help you connect with your readers on a deeper level. However, it's essential to use them judiciously, considering the context and the preferences of your readers. By mastering the art of idiomatic expressions, you can enhance the impact of your business communication.

5.3
Phrases for Different Business Situations

In the realm of business communication, employing the appropriate phrases for specific situations enhances your effectiveness and professionalism. Tailoring your language to suit the context fosters better understanding and rapport. This section delves into a variety of business situations and provides phrases that can help you navigate them with confidence and precision.

5.3.1 Meetings and Presentations

Introducing a Presentation
- Good morning/afternoon, everyone. I'm delighted to be here today to discuss...

Expressing Agreement
- I wholeheartedly agree with that point.
- I'm on board with your proposal.

Contributing to Discussion
- I'd like to add that...
- From my perspective, ...

Formal Closing
- In conclusion, I'd like to emphasize...

5.3.2 E-mail Correspondence

Requesting Information
- Could you please provide more details regarding...
- I'd appreciate it if you could clarify...

Offering Assistance
- If you need any further assistance, feel free to reach out.
- Don't hesitate to contact me if you have any questions.

Scheduling a Meeting
- Could we set up a meeting to discuss this further?
- Would you be available to meet next week?

Thanking
- Thank you for your prompt response.
- I'm grateful for your support.

5.3.3 Negotiations and Agreements

Making an Offer
- We're prepared to offer...

- Our proposal includes...

Seeking Flexibility

- Is there room for flexibility in these terms?
- Can we explore alternatives that would benefit both parties?

Expressing Willingness to Compromise

- We're open to finding a middle ground.
- Let's work together to reach a mutually agreeable solution.

Confirming Agreement

- I'm pleased to confirm that we've reached a consensus.
- Based on our discussions, we're aligned on the terms.

5.3.4 Networking and Social Events

Initiating a Conversation

- Hi, I don't believe we've had a chance to meet. I'm [Your Name].

Discussing Common Interests

- I noticed we share an interest in [topic].
- I heard you're involved in [activity], which I find intriguing.

Expressing Appreciation

- Thank you for taking the time to chat with me.
- It's been a pleasure getting to know you.

Exchanging Contact Information

- Would you mind sharing your contact details?
- Could I have your business card?

Equipping yourself with a repertoire of appropriate phrases for various business scenarios empowers you to communicate fluently and effectively. Whether it's a formal presentation, a crucial negotiation, or a networking event, selecting the right phrases demonstrates your professionalism and adaptability.

Class Activity 6: *Choose the following business scenarios and create a short role-play using the provided phrases in pairs or groups.*

1. **Meeting Scenario**

   Situation: A team meeting to discuss a new project.

   Role-play: Team members introduce themselves and summarize their project contributions.

2. **Negotiation Scenario**

   Situation: Negotiating a contract with a potential client.

   Role-play: One side makes an initial offer, the other side seeks clarification, and the two sides eventually reach an agreement.

3. **Job Interview Scenario**

   Situation: Conducting a job interview for a marketing position.

   Role-play: The interviewer asks behavioral questions, and the interviewee responds.

4. **Customer Complaint Scenario**

   Situation: Handling a customer complaint about a defective product.

   Role-play: The customer expresses dissatisfaction, and the customer service representative offers a solution.

5. **Feedback Scenario**

   Situation: Providing feedback for a colleague on a recent project.

   Role-play: One colleague gives positive feedback, and the other provides constructive feedback, and both receive feedback professionally.

6. **Presentation Scenario**

   Situation: Delivering a presentation to potential investors.

   Role-play: The presenter introduces the agenda, asks for questions, and concludes the presentation.

7. **E-mail Scenario**

   Situation: Writing a follow-up e-mail after a business meeting.

   Role-play: One colleague composes the e-mail, and the other responds professionally.

8. **Networking Scenario**

    Situation: Attending a networking event to establish professional connections.

    Role-play: Participants introduce themselves, discuss their backgrounds, and exchange contact information.

9. **Conflict Resolution Scenario**

    Situation: Mediating a conflict between two team members.

    Role-play: Two team members have a disagreement, and the mediator helps them reach a resolution.

10. **Sales Scenario**

    Situation: Making a sales pitch to a potential client.

    Role-play: The salesperson makes an offer, the client seeks clarifications, and the two sides eventually reach a decision.

Unit 6
Business Writing Formats

This chapter delves into various business writing formats and the skills required to excel in each. Whether it's composing concise e-mails, crafting formal letters, preparing informative memos, generating comprehensive reports, or formulating persuasive proposals, mastering these skills is essential for successful communication across different business contexts.

Through a combination of theory, real-world examples, exercises, and practical tips, you'll develop the proficiency needed to navigate diverse writing situations. Whether you're a seasoned professional looking to refine your skills or an aspiring business writer seeking to build a strong foundation, this chapter serves as your comprehensive guide to mastering essential business writing skills.

Let's embark on a journey to enhance your communication prowess and elevate your impact in the world of business writing.

6.1
Writing Business E-mails

In today's fast-paced business world, effective communication through e-mail is essential for professional success. Writing business e-mails requires a unique set of skills to convey your message clearly, maintain professionalism, and foster positive relationships. This section will guide you through the key elements of crafting impactful business e-mails.

6.1.1 Types of Business E-mails

In the realm of business communication, e-mails have emerged as one of the most versatile and widely used tools. They facilitate quick and efficient exchanges of information, allowing professionals to connect across distances and time zones. However, not all business e-mails are created equal. The effectiveness of an e-mail depends on its purpose, context, and the audience it targets.

Understanding the various types of business e-mails is akin to having a toolkit with different tools for different tasks. Each type serves a distinct purpose, enabling professionals to navigate diverse scenarios in the corporate world. Let's delve into some of the most common types of business e-mails and explore when and how to employ them effectively.

1. **Inquiry E-mails**

   These e-mails are the detectives of the business world. They seek information, clarity, or answers to specific questions. Inquiry e-mails are often sent when you need additional details about a product, service, job vacancy, or project.

2. **Follow-Up E-mails**

   Just as a gentle reminder can jog one's memory, follow-up e-mails serve to remind recipients about a pending action or response. They are crucial in maintaining communication flow and ensuring that tasks progress smoothly.

3. **Appreciation and Thank-You E-mails**

   Gratitude goes a long way in business relationships. These e-mails express appreciation for a favor, an assistance, or an opportunity. They help in nurturing goodwill and rapport with colleagues, clients, or partners.

4. **Formal Correspondence**

   These e-mails adhere to strict conventions of professionalism and etiquette. They are used in formal communication settings such as job applications, resignation letters, and official announcements.

5. **Informative or Announcement E-mails**

   When you have news to share, be it about a new product launch, a change in company policy, or an upcoming event, informative or announcement e-mails are your go-to-guy. They disseminate essential information to a wider audience.

6. Complaint and Issue Resolution E-mails

When problems arise, it's crucial to address them promptly and professionally. Complaint and issue resolution e-mails are used to communicate grievances, report problems, and seek resolutions.

7. Networking and Introduction E-mails

In the world of business, connections are invaluable. Networking and introduction e-mails are used to expand professional circles, connect with new contacts, or introduce oneself or a colleague to others.

Each type of business e-mail has its unique tone, structure, and purpose. As we delve deeper into this section, we will explore these types in detail, dissect their components, and offer practical guidance on when and how to employ them effectively. Remember, just as a carpenter selects the right tool for a specific task, a skilled professional chooses the right type of e-mail to achieve their communication goals.

6.1.2 Understanding the Structure of Business E-mails

Business e-mails should adhere to a clear and concise structure. Follow these guidelines to ensure your message is well-organized and easy to comprehend.

1. Subject Line

Write a descriptive subject line that summarizes the purpose of the e-mail. A compelling subject line increases the likelihood of your e-mail being read promptly. A clear and concise subject line in business e-mails is vital because it helps the recipients understand the e-mail's purpose quickly and encourages them to click and read the message. Here are some examples illustrating the importance of a clear and concise subject line:

- **Ineffective Subject Line:** "Meeting"
- **Improved Subject Line:** "Reminder: Marketing Team Meeting Tomorrow at 10 A.M."

The first subject line "Meeting" is vague and doesn't provide any context. Recipients may not know which meeting it refers to or its urgency. In contrast, the improved subject line specifies the meeting's purpose, audience ("Marketing Team"), date, and time. This clarity ensures that the recipients are well-informed and can plan accordingly.

- **Ineffective Subject Line**: "Report"
- **Improved Subject Line:** "Urgent: Quarterly Sales Report Submission Deadline—2 Days Left"

The initial subject line "Report" lacks specificity, making it unclear what kind of report is required or the urgency involved. The improved subject line not only specifies the report type ("Quarterly Sales Report") but also emphasizes its urgency by mentioning the submission deadline. This clarity prompts quicker action from the recipients.

- **Ineffective Subject Line:** "Question"
- **Improved Subject Line:** "Clarification Needed: Budget Allocation for Q4 Campaign"

The vague subject line "Question" doesn't provide any context about the inquiry. In contrast, the improved subject line highlights the specific topic ("Budget Allocation for Q4 Campaign") that requires clarification. This clarity helps the recipients understand the e-mail's content at a glance.

- **Ineffective Subject Line:** "Hello"
- **Improved Subject Line:** "Introduction: New Marketing Intern—Sarah Smith"

The subject line "Hello" provides no indication of the e-mail's purpose. However, the improved subject line clearly introduces the e-mail's content—the arrival of a new marketing intern named Sarah Smith. This makes it more likely that the recipients will click the e-mail to learn about the new team member.

- **Ineffective Subject Line:** "Update"
- **Improved Subject Line:** "Key Project Update: Revised Timeline and Milestones"

The subject line "Update" is overly generic and doesn't convey what the update is about. In contrast, the improved subject line specifies that it's about a "Key Project Update", providing the recipients with a clear understanding of the e-mail's content and its relevance to their work.

These examples demonstrate how a well-crafted subject line can make the difference between an e-mail that gets noticed and one that is easily overlooked. Clarity and conciseness in subject lines save the recipients time and ensure that the e-mail's purpose is understood immediately.

2.　Salutation

Use a formal salutation, such as "Dear [Recipient's Name]", for initial contacts. For more familiar relationships, "Hello [Recipient's Name]" or even just the recipient's name can be appropriate.

3.　Introduction

Begin with a brief introduction, stating your purpose for writing. Clearly mention any previous correspondence or context that helps the recipient understand the reason behind your e-mail. For example:

> I hope this e-mail finds you well. I wanted to follow up on our discussion during the conference last week regarding the upcoming partnership opportunity.

4.　Body

Present your main message in a structured manner. Use short paragraphs and bullet points for clarity. Elaborate on the main points, providing relevant details, facts, or explanations. For example:

> Our team has reviewed the proposal, and we're excited about the potential collaboration. The market research you provided aligns well with our goals, and we believe this partnership could significantly enhance our market presence. Here are a few key points we'd like to discuss further...

5.　Call to Action

Clearly state what you expect the recipients to do after reading the e-mail. Whether it's a response, a decision, or an action, make your request explicit. For example:

> Could you please provide more details about the projected timeline for implementation? Additionally, we'd like to discuss the terms and conditions of the proposed revenue-sharing model.

6. Closing

Use a formal closing phrase, such as "Sincerely" or "Best regards", followed by your name. If appropriate, you can include your job title and contact information. For example:

> Thank you for considering our proposal. We look forward to your insights on these points.
>
> Best regards, [Your Name]
>
> Marketing Manager
>
> Contact: [Your E-mail] | [Your Phone Number]

6.1.3 Tone and Language

Maintaining a professional and courteous tone is crucial in business e-mails.

1. Formality

Adapt your level of formality based on your relationship with the recipient. Keep it more formal for new contacts or superiors and slightly more relaxed for colleagues and familiar contacts.

The following e-mail is an example of introducing oneself and his or her company's services to a prospective client, using an appropriate level of formality.

> Subject: Introduction and Overview of Our Services
>
> Dear Mr. John,
>
> I trust this e-mail finds you well. My name is Nancy, and I am thrilled to introduce myself as a representative of BluePeak Technologies. We specialize in providing tailored solutions that empower businesses to achieve their goals with utmost efficiency and innovation.
>
> Allow me to give you a brief overview of our services. At BluePeak Technologies, we pride ourselves on offering a comprehensive suite of strategic consulting, technology implementation, and project management solutions. With a proven track record of delivering results for clients across various industries, we have cultivated a deep understanding of the challenges that businesses like yours encounter.
>
> Our team comprises seasoned professionals who bring a wealth of expertise to the table. We are dedicated to partnering with our clients to develop customized

strategies that drive growth, enhance operational excellence, and foster a competitive edge in the market. Our commitment to quality and client satisfaction has earned us recognition as a trusted partner in the industry.

I would be delighted to discuss your specific needs and explore how BluePeak Technologies can contribute to your success. Please let me know a convenient time for a brief call or meeting, and I will ensure that our team is fully prepared to address your inquiries.

Thank you for considering BluePeak Technologies as a potential collaborator. We look forward to the opportunity to demonstrate the value we can bring to your organization. Should you have any questions or require additional information, please don't hesitate to reach out.

Best regards,

Nancy May

Director of Marketing and Communications

E-mail: nancy.may@innovadesign.com

Phone: +1 (555) 123-4567

Office Address: 1200 Riverside Drive, Suite 200, New York, NY 10011

2. Clarity

Use clear and straightforward language. Avoid jargon, acronyms, and overly technical terms that the recipient might not understand.

The following e-mail is an example of writing a technical explanation from one's field in a way that a non-expert can understand, and use it in an e-mail to his or her colleagues.

Subject: Simplified Explanation of Project Algorithm

Dear Hellen,

I hope this e-mail finds you well. I want to provide you with a clear understanding of the algorithm we're implementing for our upcoming project, "Project XYZ", without diving into technical jargon.

In essence, our algorithm is like a super-smart guide that helps the computer make decisions based on a large amount of data. Imagine it as a chef who uses various ingredients to create a delicious dish. Our algorithm takes different pieces of information and combines them to give us useful insights.

Instead of using complex mathematical equations, we've designed the algorithm to follow simple steps, like a recipe. These steps help the computer sort through information, identify patterns, and make predictions. Just like a weather forecast predicts if it will rain tomorrow based on past data, our algorithm predicts specific outcomes based on the data we input.

The exciting part is that this algorithm gets better over time. It learns from its mistakes and successes, much like how we learn from our experiences. As we feed it more data, it becomes more accurate at making predictions, which is crucial for the success of "Project XYZ".

I hope this explanation gives you a clearer picture of our project's core technology. If you have any questions or want to discuss it further, please don't hesitate to reach out.

Best regards,

Nancy May

Director of Marketing and Communications

E-mail: nancy.may@innovadesign.com

Phone: +1 (555) 123-4567

Office Address: 1200 Riverside Drive, Suite 200, New York, NY 10011

3. Politeness

Be polite and respectful, even when discussing sensitive topics. Use polite language when making requests and expressing opinions.

The following e-mail is an example of declining an invitation to a networking event while expressing appreciation for the invitation.

Subject: Re: Invitation to Networking Event

Dear Mrs. Jackson,

I hope this e-mail finds you well. I want to extend my sincere appreciation for inviting me to the upcoming networking event on May 25, 2024. Your thoughtfulness in considering me for this event means a lot.

Unfortunately, due to a prior commitment that coincides with the event, I will not be able to attend. While I'm disappointed to miss out on what I'm sure will be a valuable and enjoyable opportunity, I'm truly grateful for the invitation.

I believe in the power of networking and the exchange of ideas, and I'm eager to connect with professionals in our industry. I hope that our paths will cross at future events, and I look forward to the possibility of meeting you and your colleagues on another occasion.

Once again, thank you for thinking of me and including me in the event. I wish you a successful and productive networking event.

Best regards,

Nancy May

Director of Marketing and Communications

E-mail: nancy.may@innovadesign.com

Phone: +1 (555) 123-4567

Office Address: 1200 Riverside Drive, Suite 200, New York, NY 10011

4. Conciseness and Brevity

In business e-mails, brevity is key. Busy professionals appreciate concise e-mails that get to the point quickly. Here's how to achieve brevity: trim unnecessary details. That is, focus on the essential information and omit irrelevant details that can make the e-mail lengthy.

The following is an example of rewriting an e-mail, making it more concise while retaining all essential information.

Original E-mail	Revised E-mail
Subject: Follow-Up on Project Proposal Meeting	Subject: Project Proposal Follow-Up
Dear Mr. Smith,	Hi Mr. Smith,
I hope this e-mail finds you well. I want to follow up on our recent project proposal meeting that took place on March 20, 2023. It was a pleasure discussing our proposed collaboration to enhance your company's marketing strategy.	I hope this e-mail finds you well. Following our project proposal meeting on March 20, 2023, I'd like to reiterate our enthusiasm for the collaboration to enhance your marketing strategy.
During the meeting, we covered various aspects of the proposed project, including the scope, timeline, and	During the meeting, we discussed the project scope and timeline, and how to address potential challenges. Our experience aligns with your goals,

deliverables. We also touched on the potential challenges and how we plan to address them. I'm excited about the potential of this partnership and believe that our expertise aligns well with your goals.

I wanted to express our commitment to delivering high-quality results that exceed your expectations. We are confident that our team's experience in similar projects will contribute to the success of this endeavor. Please feel free to reach out if you have any further questions or require additional information.

Thank you for considering our proposal, and I look forward to the opportunity to work together. Please let me know a suitable time for our next steps, whether it's another meeting or any additional information you may need.

Best regards,

Nancy May

Director of Marketing and Communications

E-mail: nancy.may@innovadesign. com

Phone: +1 (555) 123-4567

Office Address: 1200 Riverside Drive, Suite 200, New York, NY 10011

and we're committed to exceeding expectations.

If you have questions or need more info, feel free to ask. Looking forward to our next steps—another meeting or information sharing. Thanks for considering our proposal.

Best,

Nancy May

Director of Marketing and Communications

E-mail: nancy.may@innovadesign. com

Phone: +1 (555) 123-4567

Office Address: 1200 Riverside Drive, Suite 200, New York, NY 10011

5. Repetition Prevention

Be mindful of repeating information or rephrasing the same points multiple times.

The following is an example of rewriting an e-mail, eliminating redundancy while preserving the message's clarity.

Original E-mail	Revised E-mail
Subject: Team Meeting Agenda for Monday, August 21st	Subject: Team Meeting Agenda—Monday, August 21st
Dear Team,	Dear Team,
I hope this e-mail finds you well. I want to remind everyone about our upcoming team meeting scheduled for Monday, August 21st, at 10:00 a.m. During this meeting, we will be discussing the project updates that have taken place over the past week. We will also be going over the progress made on the current project and any potential roadblocks that need to be addressed.	I hope this e-mail finds you well. Our team meeting is just around the corner—scheduled for Monday, August 21st, at 10:00 a.m. During this session, we'll cover a range of critical topics:
In addition to discussing the project updates and progress, we will also be touching upon the upcoming tasks that need to be completed. We will be assigning responsibilities for these tasks and discussing the deadlines that need to be met.	• Project Updates: Let's review the developments of the past week, ensuring we're all up to date. • Progress and Roadblocks: We'll assess our current project's advancement and address any potential challenges we're encountering. • Upcoming Tasks: We'll discuss the pending tasks, delegate responsibilities, and set clear deadlines.

Please make sure to mark your calendars for this important team meeting. Your presence is crucial as we need to ensure that everyone is on the same page regarding the project's status and future steps.

Looking forward to our productive discussion on Monday.

Best regards,

Nancy May

Director of Marketing and Communications

E-mail: nancy.may@innovadesign.com

Phone: +1 (555) 123-4567

Office Address: 1200 Riverside Drive, Suite 200, New York, NY 10011

Your attendance is essential as we seek alignment on the project's status and next steps. Please make sure to mark your calendars accordingly.

Looking forward to our productive discussion on Monday.

Best regards,

Nancy May

Director of Marketing and Communications

E-mail: nancy.may@innovadesign.com

Phone: +1 (555) 123-4567

Office Address: 1200 Riverside Drive, Suite 200, New York, NY 10011

6.1.4 Professional E-mail Etiquette

Mastering proper e-mail etiquette is vital for leaving a positive impression on the recipient.

1. Response Time

Aim to respond promptly to e-mails, especially if they require urgent attention. Acknowledge the receipt of the e-mail even if you can't provide a detailed response immediately.

2. Proofreading

Before sending it, proofread your e-mail for grammar, spelling, and punctuation errors. Typos can negatively impact your professional image.

Class Activity 1: *Proofread the following e-mail on the left and write the new e-mail on the right.*

Original E-mail	**Proofread E-mail**
Subject: Urgent: Missng Reports for Q4	
Dear Johanna,	
I hope this finds you well. I'm reaching out to remind you that we are still awaiting the delivery of the Q4 reports. As per our previus discussions, these were suposed to be submitted by last Friday, but we have yet to recieve them. This is causing a significant delay in our auditing process, and it's critcal that we get these documents as soon as posible.	
Additionally, there have been some concerns regarding the accuracy of the data presented in the Q3 reports. It would be beneficial if you could double-check these figures to ensure their acuracy before finalizing the Q4 reports.	
Please let me know if you encounter any issues or if there's anything you need from my side to expedite this process. We greatly appreciate your immediate attention to this matter.	
Best Regards,	
Roy	
Sales Manager	
Roy_Lin@yahoo.com	

3. Attachments

Clearly indicate any attachments you've included in the e-mail and make sure they are relevant to the message.

The following is an example of sending an e-mail to a team member, attaching a presentation file, and ensuring the mention of the attachment in the body of the e-mail.

Subject: Presentation Review and Input

Dear Smith,

I hope this e-mail finds you well. As we're moving ahead with the project, I want to share the latest version of our presentation for the upcoming client meeting. Your insights and feedback would be invaluable in making it a success.

Please find the attached presentation file named "ClientMeeting_Presentation. pptx". Kindly take a moment to review it and share your thoughts. Your input on the content, flow, and visuals will greatly contribute to refining our message.

Your expertise is highly regarded, and I believe your input will elevate the quality of our presentation. Feel free to jot down any notes directly in the file or reply to this e-mail with your suggestions.

I appreciate your prompt attention to this matter. Let's aim to finalize the presentation by June 6, 2023 to allow ample time for any adjustments.

Thank you for your dedication to this project. I'm looking forward to your insights.

Best regards,

Nancy May

Director of Marketing and Communications

E-mail: nancy.may@innovadesign.com

Phone: +1 (555) 123-4567

Office Address: 1200 Riverside Drive, Suite 200, New York, NY 10011

Attachment: ClientMeeting_Presentation.pptx

---

4. E-mail Follow-Up

When necessary, follow up on your initial e-mail. Wait a reasonable amount of time before sending a follow-up e-mail. This varies depending on the urgency of your message and your relationship with the recipient.

The following e-mail is an example of following up on a client's inquiry about a proposal after a week of no response.

Subject: Follow-Up: Proposal Inquiry

Dear Mr. Collin,

I hope this e-mail finds you well. I want to touch base regarding the proposal we sent over last week. We're excited about the potential partnership and the value we believe our collaboration could bring to HorizonWave.

I understand that schedules can get busy, and I want to ensure that our proposal receives the attention it deserves. If you've had a chance to review it, I'd love to hear your initial thoughts. Your insights are vital as we tailor our solutions to your specific needs.

If there are any questions or additional information you require, please don't hesitate to reach out. We're here to provide clarity and address any concerns you may have.

Our team is eager to move forward and explore how we can make this partnership a reality. Please let us know how you'd like to proceed or if you'd like to schedule a call to discuss the proposal in more detail.

Thank you for considering us as a potential partner. We appreciate the opportunity and look forward to your response.

Best regards,

Nancy May

Director of Marketing and Communications

E-mail: nancy.may@innovadesign.com

Phone: +1 (555) 123-4567

Office Address: 1200 Riverside Drive, Suite 200, New York, NY 10011

5. Polite Reminder

Politely reference the initial e-mail and kindly request an update or response, if applicable.

The following is an example of a follow-up e-mail requesting feedback on a recent project proposal while expressing his or her eagerness to move forward.

Subject: Seeking Your Feedback on Project Proposal

Dear Ms. Yuan,

I hope this e-mail finds you well. I want to follow up on the project proposal we submitted last week. We're eager to hear your thoughts and feedback, as your insights are essential in shaping our next steps.

The proposed project aligns closely with your objectives, and we're excited about the potential impact it could have on Visionary Flux. Your perspective is valuable in ensuring that our solutions address your unique needs effectively.

If you've had a chance to review the proposal, we'd greatly appreciate any comments or suggestions you might have. Whether it's about the scope, deliverables, or any other aspect, your input will help us refine the proposal and tailor it even more precisely to your requirements.

We believe that this partnership has great potential, and we're eager to move forward in a direction that aligns with your vision. If there are any specific details you'd like to discuss or if you have any questions, please feel free to reach out.

Thank you for considering us as your partner for this project. We're excited about the possibility of working together and creating a successful outcome. Your feedback will guide us in shaping the project to meet and exceed your expectations.

Looking forward to your response.

Best regards,

Nancy May

Director of Marketing and Communications

E-mail: nancy.may@innovadesign.com

Phone: +1 (555) 123-4567

Office Address: 1200 Riverside Drive, Suite 200, New York, NY 10011

6. Acknowledging Responses

Always acknowledge and thank the recipient for his or her responses or actions.

The following e-mail is an example of responding to a colleague's e-mail confirming attendance at a meeting, expressing gratitude for his or her prompt response.

Subject: Re: Meeting Confirmation

Hi William,

Thank you for your swift response. I appreciate your confirmation to attend the meeting scheduled for 3 p.m., March 8, 2024.

Your commitment to our team's collaboration is truly valued. Your input will be crucial in advancing our project and ensuring its success.

If you have any questions or points you'd like to discuss during the meeting, please don't hesitate to let me know in advance. Looking forward to a productive discussion.

Thanks again for your prompt confirmation.

Best regards,

Nancy May

Director of Marketing and Communications

E-mail: nancy.may@innovadesign.com

Phone: +1 (555) 123-4567

Office Address: 1200 Riverside Drive, Suite 200, New York, NY 10011

By mastering the art of writing business e-mails, you'll enhance your professional communication skills and establish yourself as an effective and reliable communicator in the business world. Remember to practice these principles and adjust your approach based on the specific context and recipient.

6.2
Writing Business Letters

In the digital age, business letters remain a powerful tool for formal communication. Whether you're corresponding with clients, partners, or colleagues, crafting effective business letters can leave a lasting impression. This section will guide you through the nuances of writing impactful business letters that convey professionalism, clarity, and purpose.

6.2.1 Common Types of Business Letters and Their Purposes

In the realm of business communication, various types of business letters serve distinct purposes. Understanding when and how to use these letter formats is crucial for effective communication. Below, we explore some common types of business letters and their specific purposes.

1. **Cover Letters**

Cover letters are typically submitted along with job applications and resumés. They introduce the applicant to the potential employer, highlighting qualifications, skills, and motivation for the position. The key elements include introduction, explanation of qualifications, expression of interest, and closing.

2. Inquiry Letters

Inquiry letters are used to request information or seek clarification on specific matters. They are often sent to companies, institutions, or individuals to gather details about products, services, or opportunities. The key elements include introduction, purpose of inquiry, specific questions or requests, and contact information.

3. Complaint Letters

Complaint letters are composed when a customer or client encounters issues with a product, service, or experience. They aim to express dissatisfaction and seek resolution or compensation. The key elements include: explanation of the problem, details of the incident, requested action or resolution, and contact information.

4. Thank-You Letters

Thank-you letters are expressions of gratitude and appreciation. They are used to acknowledge favors, assistance, gifts, interviews, or opportunities. These letters help build and maintain positive relationships. The key elements include expressions of thanks, specific details about what is being appreciated, goodwill messages, and closing.

5. Sales and Marketing Letters

Sales and marketing letters are instrumental in promoting products, services, or events. They aim to persuade recipients to take action, such as making a purchase, attending an event, or subscribing to a service. The key elements include introduction, description of offerings, benefits, call to action, and contact information.

6. Formal Correspondence

Formal correspondence includes letters such as resignation letters, acceptance of job offers, or official announcements. These letters adhere to strict conventions of professionalism and are used for formal documentation. The key elements include salutation, concise and clear messages, adherence to formal tone, and contact information.

7. Information or Announcement Letters

Information or announcement letters disseminate important news, updates, or information within an organization or to external stakeholders. These letters keep stakeholders informed and aligned. The key elements include clear announcement or information, details, relevant dates, and contact information.

Each type of business letter serves a unique purpose, and mastering them is essential for effective communication in the business world. By understanding when and how to use these letter formats and tailoring their content to suit the intended audience and purpose, you can enhance your written communication skills and achieve business goals effectively.

6.2.2 Understanding the Structure

Business letters adhere to a standardized structure, ensuring that your message is well-organized and easy to navigate. The standardized structure usually includes:

- **Sender's Information:** Include your name, job title, company name, address, and contact details at the top of the letter.

- **Date:** Indicate the date on which the letter is written, aligning it to business conventions.

- **Recipient's Information:** Provide the recipient's name, job title, company name, address, and contact details.

- **Salutation:** Address the recipient with a formal salutation, such as "Dear [Recipient's Last Name]", followed by a comma.

- **Introduction:** Begin with a concise introduction that states the purpose of the letter and establishes context.

- **Body:** Present the main content of the letter in clear and coherent paragraphs. Elaborate on key points and provide relevant details.

- **Closing:** Conclude the letter with a courteous closing phrase, such as "Sincerely" or "Yours faithfully", followed by your signature and typed name.

- **Enclosures:** If you're including additional documents with the letter, list them under the word "Enclosures" at the bottom of the letter.

The following is an example of a business letter.

[Your Name]

[Your Title]

[Your Company Name]

[Your Address]

[City, State, ZIP]

[Your E-mail]

[Your Phone Number]

[Date]

[Recipient's Name]

[Recipient's Title]

[Recipient's Company Name]

[Recipient's Address]

[City, State, ZIP]

Dear [Recipient's Last Name],

I hope this letter finds you well. I am writing to express my sincere appreciation for the opportunity to collaborate with [Recipient's Company Name] on the [Project Name]. I wanted to provide you with an update on the progress and share some exciting developments.

Since the inception of the project on [Project Start Date], our team has been dedicated to ensuring its success. We have carefully analyzed the project requirements and have made substantial progress in the initial phase. Our focus has been on understanding the specific needs of [Recipient's Company Name] and aligning our strategies to meet those needs effectively.

I am pleased to inform you that we have successfully completed the research and analysis phase, which has provided us with valuable insights into the market trends and consumer preferences. This information will be pivotal in shaping our approach for the upcoming phases of the project.

As we move forward, we are confident that our collective efforts will result in a solution that not only meets but exceeds your expectations. Our team is committed to maintaining open lines of communication and collaborating closely with your team to ensure a seamless execution of the project.

Enclosed with this letter, you will find a detailed report highlighting the progress we have made so far. We believe that transparency is key to a successful partnership, and we are eager to receive your feedback and insights on the report.

Please feel free to reach out at [Your Phone Number] or [Your E-mail] if you have any questions, concerns, or suggestions. We highly value your input and look forward to your guidance as we continue to work together on the [Project Name].

Thank you once again for entrusting us with this project. We are truly excited about the journey ahead and the positive impact our collaboration will have on [Recipient's Company Name].

Sincerely,
[Your Signature]
[Your Typed Name]
[Your Title]
[Your Company Name]
[Your Contact Information]
Enclosures: Progress Report

6.2.3 Tone and Language

The tone of business letters varies based on the formality of your relationship with the recipient. A formal tone means you should maintain a professional and respectful style, using appropriate language and avoiding colloquialisms. Be concise while ensuring the letter conveys the necessary information clearly. Avoid verbosity and unnecessary details.

6.2.4 Addressing Concerns

Addressing specific concerns effectively in business letters is essential.

1. Complaints

When you address a complaint, focus on the issue and its potential solutions rather than placing blame. You are supposed to maintain a diplomatic and respectful tone.

The following e-mail is an example of complaint.

[Your Name]
[Your Address]
[City, State, ZIP]
[Your E-mail]
[Your Phone Number]
[Date]

[Company Name]

[Customer Service Department]
[Company Address]
[City, State, ZIP]

Dear [Company Name],

I am writing to express my dissatisfaction with a recent experience I had with your products and services. I believe it is important to bring this matter to your attention in the hope that it can be resolved in a satisfactory manner.

On [Date], I purchased a [Product Name] from your store, and unfortunately, the product did not meet my expectations. The [specific issue you encountered, such as product defect or poor quality] has left me disappointed and frustrated.

As a long-time customer of [Company Name], I have always held your products in high regard and recommended them to friends and family. However, this recent experience has caused me to question the quality and reliability of your offerings.

I kindly request that you take immediate action to address this issue. I believe in your commitment to customer satisfaction and hope that you will work towards resolving this matter promptly. I am attaching a copy of the purchase receipt for your reference.

I value the relationship I have had with your company over the years and believe that by addressing this concern, you can help restore my confidence in your brand. I am open to a constructive resolution that would leave me satisfied with the outcome.

I would appreciate a prompt response to this letter and a clear plan of action to rectify the situation. You can reach me at [Your Phone Number] or [Your E-mail] to discuss this matter further.

Thank you for your attention to this matter. I look forward to your timely response and a resolution that restores my faith in the quality and service your company has been known for.

Sincerely,

[Your Signature]

[Your Typed Name]

2. Requests

Clearly state your request and provide relevant background information to help the recipient understand its significance.

The following e-mail is an example of request.

[Your Name]
[Your Address]
[City, State, ZIP]
[Your E-mail]
[Your Phone Number]
[Date]

[Recipient's Name]
[Recipient's Title]
[Recipient's Company Name]
[Recipient's Address]
[City, State, ZIP]

Dear [Recipient's Last Name],

I hope this letter finds you well. I am writing to kindly request [specific request you are making]. I believe that your expertise and support would greatly contribute to [explain the purpose or benefit of the request].

The reason I am reaching out to you is that I am aware of your extensive knowledge and experience in [relevant field or area of expertise]. Your insights have proven invaluable in similar situations, and I am confident that your input can help us achieve [specific goal or outcome].

I understand that your time is valuable, and I greatly appreciate your consideration of my request. Your support would make a significant difference in [describe the impact or outcome of your request]. If you require any additional information or context to better understand the situation, please do not hesitate to contact me.

I am hopeful that you will find merits in this request and will be willing to contribute your expertise. Your involvement would mean a lot to me personally and to [explain who else would benefit from your request].

Thank you for considering my request. I look forward to hearing from you at your earliest convenience. You can reach me at [Your Phone Number] or [Your E-mail] if you have any questions or if you need further information.

Once again, thank you for your time and consideration.

Sincerely,

[Your Signature]

[Your Typed Name]

3. Acknowledgments

Express gratitude when acknowledging the receipt of payments, documents, or other contributions from the recipient.

The following e-mail is an example of acknowledgment.

[Your Name]
[Your Title]
[Your Company Name]
[Your Address]
[City, State, ZIP]
[Your E-mail]
[Your Phone Number]
[Date]

[Recipient's Name]
[Recipient's Title]
[Recipient's Company Name]
[Recipient's Address]
[City, State, ZIP]

Dear [Recipient's Last Name],

I hope this letter finds you well. I am writing to express my sincere gratitude for your prompt and valuable contribution to [describe the contribution, e.g., the recent payment/documents].

Your swift response and cooperation are greatly appreciated, and they demonstrate your commitment to our partnership. Your [payment/documents] have been received and processed successfully, and we are pleased to acknowledge the completion of this transaction.

The [payment/documents] play a significant role in [describe the impact or purpose of the contribution, e.g., supporting the project/initiative]. Your contribution ensures that we can move forward with confidence and achieve our shared objectives.

Please accept our heartfelt thanks for your timely response and dedication to our collaboration. We value your continued support and look forward to further strengthening our partnership.

If you have any questions or require additional information, please feel free to reach out to me at [Your Phone Number] or [Your E-mail]. Your feedback is always welcome and helps us improve our services.

Once again, thank you for your contribution. We are truly grateful for your ongoing partnership.

Sincerely,

[Your Signature]

[Your Typed Name]

4. Follow-Up and Thank-You Letters

Following up or expressing gratitude through business letters strengthens relationships. You can send follow-up letters after meetings, discussions, or negotiations to summarize key points and outline agreed-upon actions. Thank-you letters are used to express gratitude for business opportunities, referrals, collaborations, etc.

6.2.5 Tailoring for Different Scenarios

Adapt your letter-writing approach to various scenarios.

1. Sales and Marketing Letters

Promote products, services, or events effectively by showcasing their benefits and catering to the recipient's needs.

The following is an example of a sales and marketing letter.

[Your Name]

[Your Title]

[Your Company Name]

[Your Address]

[City, State, ZIP]

[Your E-mail]

[Your Phone Number]

[Date]

[Recipient's Name]

[Recipient's Title]

[Recipient's Company Name]

[Recipient's Address]

[City, State, ZIP]

Dear [Recipient's Last Name],

I hope this letter finds you well. I am excited to introduce you to our latest offering that I believe aligns perfectly with [Recipient's Company Name]'s goals and aspirations. Allow me to present to you the [Product/Service Name].

In today's dynamic business landscape, staying ahead requires innovation and efficiency. The [Product/Service Name] is designed to empower companies like [Recipient's Company Name] to streamline their operations, boost productivity, and achieve tangible results.

Here's how the [Product/Service Name] can benefit your organization:

- Increased Efficiency: Our [Product/Service Name] optimizes processes, reducing manual efforts and ensuring tasks are completed more efficiently.
- Data-Driven Insights: Our [Product/Service Name] can gain valuable insights into your operations with advanced analytics, enabling informed decision-making and improved strategies.
- Seamless Integration: The [Product/Service Name] seamlessly integrates into your existing systems, ensuring a smooth transition without disruptions.
- Customizable Solutions: We understand that every business is unique. The [Product/Service Name] offers customizable features tailored to your specific needs.

To provide you with a deeper understanding of the benefits and features, I have enclosed a brochure that provides an overview of the [Product/Service Name]. I would also be delighted to arrange a demonstration tailored to your organization's needs.

At [Your Company Name], we take pride in offering innovative solutions that drive growth and success. We are confident that the [Product/Service Name] can become an integral part of [Recipient's Company Name]'s journey toward excellence.

Thank you for considering the [Product/Service Name]. I look forward to the opportunity to discuss how this solution can address your unique challenges and contribute to your ongoing success. Please feel free to contact me at [Your Phone Number] or [Your E-mail].

Sincerely,

[Your Signature]

[Your Typed Name]

2. Invitation Letters

Invite clients or partners to events, conferences, or seminars by clearly outlining the purpose and benefits of attending.

The following is an example of an invitation letter.

[Your Name]
[Your Title]
[Your Company Name]
[Your Address]
[City, State, ZIP]
[Your E-mail]
[Your Phone Number]
[Date]

[Recipient's Name]
[Recipient's Title]
[Recipient's Company Name]
[Recipient's Address]
[City, State, ZIP]

Dear [Recipient's Last Name],

I am delighted to extend a warm invitation to you and your esteemed team to attend the [Event/Conference/Seminar] hosted by [Your Company Name]. This event promises to be a transformative experience, offering insights and networking opportunities that can significantly benefit [Recipient's Company Name].

Event Details:

- Date: [Date]
- Time: [Time]
- Venue: [Venue]

At [Your Company Name], we believe in the power of collaboration and knowledge sharing. The [Event/Conference/Seminar] is designed to provide attendees with a deep dive into [Key Themes or Topics]. Our carefully curated lineup of speakers and interactive sessions will explore the latest industry trends, best practices, and innovative solutions.

Here's why you should consider joining us:

- Expert Insights: Gain valuable insights from industry experts and thought leaders who will share their experiences and strategies for success.
- Networking Opportunities: Connect with professionals from diverse industries, fostering valuable relationships and potential partnerships.
- Interactive Workshops: Participate in hands-on workshops that will equip you with actionable skills and knowledge to implement in your organization.
- Exclusive Access: As our valued guest, you'll have exclusive access to materials and resources shared during the event.

To ensure you make the most of this opportunity, we have attached an agenda that outlines the sessions, topics, and speakers. We encourage you to share this invitation with your team members who would also benefit from attending.

Please confirm your attendance by [Reservation Date] to ensure that we can reserve a seat for you and your team. You can RSVP by replying to this e-mail or contacting [Your Contact Details].

We are excited about the potential collaboration between [Your Company Name] and [Recipient's Company Name]. Your presence at the [Event/Conference/Seminar] will contribute to the success of this event and further strengthen our partnership.

Thank you for considering our invitation. We look forward to welcoming you and your team at the event.

Sincerely,

[Your Signature]

[Your Typed Name]

Class Activity 2: *Read the following excerpts, which illustrate some common issues in business letter writing, such as vagueness, informality, lack of specificity, and unnecessary directness. Then rewrite these excerpts to make them more effective, professional, and clear while maintaining the intended message and tone.*

1. I am writing to inform you that your payment is overdue.

2. Our product is great. You should try it.

3. I want to discuss the project with you.

4. Your feedback is necessary.

5. We have a special offer for our valued customers.

6. Our service is top-notch.

7. The meeting will take place on Friday.

8. You have made a mistake.

9. I need a response by tomorrow.

6.3
Writing Memos

In the fast-paced world of business communication, memos serve as concise and effective tools for conveying important information within an organization. Whether sharing updates, announcing decisions, or requesting actions, writing clear and well-structured memos is essential for effective internal communication. This section will guide you through the process of crafting impactful memos that capture attention and drive action.

6.3.1 Understanding the Purpose

Memos, or memorandums, are brief written messages designed to transmit information efficiently within a company. They are commonly used for the following purposes:

- **Sharing updates**, which involves communicating changes, progress reports, or project milestones to relevant team members.

- **Making announcements**, which includes distributing important announcements, such as policy changes, upcoming events, or new initiatives.

- **Requesting actions**, which means outlining tasks, assignments, or actions that recipients need to complete.

- **Providing recommendations**, which offers insights and suggestions on specific matters that require attention.

6.3.2 Structuring Your Memo

A well-structured memo ensures that your message is easily understood. It should include the following elements:

- **Heading:** Include the word "Memo" or "Memorandum" at the top, followed by the date and the names of both the sender and the recipient.

- **Subject Line:** Write a concise and clear subject line that summarizes the purpose of the memo.

- **Opening:** Begin with a brief introduction that provides context for the memo's content.

- **Body:** Present the main content of the memo in short and focused paragraphs. Use headings, bullet points, or numbered lists to organize information.

- **Conclusion:** Summarize the key points and indicate any specific actions or follow-up steps required.

- **Closing:** End with a closing statement, such as "Thank you for your attention" or "Please feel free to contact me with any questions".

- **Sender's Contact Information:** Include your contact details for recipients to reach out if needed.

The following is an example of memo.

Memo

Date: August 16, 2023

To: All Department Heads

From: Jane Smith, HR Manager

Subject: New Employee Onboarding Process

Dear Department Heads,

I hope this memo finds you well. I am writing to inform you about the enhancements we are making to our new employee onboarding process, effective September 1, 2023.

Introduction

As our company continues to grow, it is essential that we provide a seamless onboarding experience for our new hires. This not only ensures their smooth integration into our team but also contributes to higher employee engagement and productivity.

Body

- Streamlined Onboarding Steps: We have restructured the onboarding process to be more streamlined and efficient. Each new employee will receive a personalized onboarding plan that outlines the necessary steps, training, and introductions.

- Assigned Onboarding Buddy: To facilitate a warm welcome, each new employee will be assigned an onboarding buddy from their respective department. This buddy will be responsible for answering questions, providing guidance, and assisting with the integration process.
- Enhanced Orientation Day: We are introducing an extended orientation day that covers company values, culture, policies, and essential tools. This will provide new employees with a comprehensive understanding of our organization.
- Feedback Loop: We value continuous improvement. We encourage department heads to share feedback on the onboarding process. Your insights will be invaluable in refining our procedures over time.

Conclusion

We believe that these enhancements will create a positive onboarding experience and contribute to long-term employee satisfaction. Please share this memo with your teams and ensure that all relevant members are informed about the changes.

Closing

Thank you for your support in ensuring a smooth transition for our new employees. If you have any questions or need further information, please do not hesitate to contact me at [Your E-mail] or [Your Phone Number].

Sincerely,

Jane Smith

HR Manager

[Your Company Name]

[Your Contact Information]

6.3.3 Tone and Language

Maintain a professional and concise tone in your memos. You should follow the principles of:

- **Clarity:** Use clear and direct language to ensure recipients understand the message without ambiguity.
- **Brevity:** Keep your memo succinct and focused on the main points.
- **Avoiding Jargon:** If using technical terms or acronyms, provide explanations to ensure clarity.

6.3.4　Visual Elements

Utilize visual elements to enhance readability and emphasize important points. They include:

- **Headings and Subheadings:** Organize content using headings and subheadings to guide the readers through the memo.
- **Bullet Points and Lists:** Present information in bullet points or numbered lists to convey key details efficiently.

The following is an example of memo with bullet points.

Memo

Date: [Date]
From: [Your Name]
To: [Recipient's Name]
Subject: Update on [Project Name]

Dear [Recipient's Name],
I wanted to provide you with an update on the progress of the [Project Name]. As of [Current Date], we have successfully completed [Milestone Achieved] and are on track to meet our goals.
Key Highlights:
- [Brief Description of Milestone]
- [Summary of Achievements]

Looking ahead, our next steps include [Upcoming Milestones or Tasks]. If you have any questions or require additional information, please do not hesitate to reach out.
Thank you for your ongoing support and collaboration.
Best regards,
[Your Name]
[Your Title]
[Your Contact Information]

By practicing memo writing, you will develop the skills necessary to communicate essential information efficiently within your organization.

Class Activity 3: *Write a memo to your team announcing an upcoming company-wide training session. The memo should include the details, such as the date, time, location, and topics covered, emphasize the importance of participation, and outline any preparations team members need to make.*

Class Activity 4: *Edit the following memo to enhance its clarity and effectiveness while maintaining a professional tone.*

Memorandum

To: All Staff
From: [Your Name]
Date: [Date]
Re: Important Meeting

Please be informed that there will be a meeting next week. Your attendance is expected. The meeting will be held on [Date] at [Time]. We will discuss important matters. Please come prepared.

Thank you.

6.4
Writing Business Reports

Business reports are essential tools for communicating detailed information, analyses, and recommendations within an organization. These reports provide insights into various aspects of business operations, helping decision-makers make informed choices. This section will guide you through the process of creating effective and impactful business reports that convey complex information clearly and concisely.

6.4.1 Common Types of Business Reports and Their Purposes

Business reports are essential tools for communication within organizations and with external stakeholders. They come in various types, each designed for specific purposes. Here are some common types of business reports and their respective purposes.

1. Research Reports

Research reports are generated after a thorough investigation and analysis of a particular topic or problem. They provide insights, findings, and recommendations based on empirical data. The use cases include market research reports, industry analysis reports, and scientific research reports.

2. Annual Reports

Annual reports offer a comprehensive overview of a company's financial performance, achievements, and future outlook. They are crucial for shareholders, investors, and regulatory authorities. The use cases include corporate annual reports, financial statements, and sustainability reports.

3. Project Reports

Project reports document the progress, status, and outcomes of a specific project. They often include project goals, timelines, budgets, and lessons learned. The use cases include project status reports, post-project evaluation reports, and project proposal reports.

4. Feasibility Studies

Feasibility study reports assess the viability and potential risks of a proposed project or business venture. They help stakeholders make informed decisions. The use cases include market feasibility studies, financial feasibility reports, and technical feasibility reports.

5. Business Proposals

Business proposals aim to persuade recipients to take specific actions, such as investing, partnering, or approving a project. They present a compelling case for a proposed initiative. The use cases include investment proposals, partnership proposals, and project proposals.

6. Technical Reports

Technical reports provide detailed information on technical topics, such as product specifications, research findings, or engineering solutions. They cater to a specialized audience. The use cases include engineering reports, scientific research papers, and technical manuals.

7. Strategic Plans

Strategic plans outline an organization's long-term goals, objectives, and strategies for achieving them. They provide a roadmap for future growth and development. The use cases include business strategic plans, marketing plans, and growth strategies.

8. Compliance and Audit Reports

Compliance and audit reports ensure that an organization adheres to legal and regulatory requirements. They verify and document internal controls and processes. The use cases include internal audit reports, compliance reports, and financial audit reports.

9. Sales and Marketing Reports

Sales and marketing reports track and analyze sales performance, customer behavior, and marketing campaigns. They inform marketing strategies and sales forecasts. The use cases include sales performance reports, market research reports, marketing and campaign reports.

10. Executive Summaries

Executive summaries provide condensed versions of longer reports or documents, offering key findings and recommendations to busy executives. They are usually included in various types of reports to facilitate quick decision-making.

The choice of report type depends on the specific communication needs and objectives of an organization or project. Each type of report serves a distinct role in conveying information, facilitating decision-making, and ensuring transparency and accountability within the business environment.

6.4.2 Understanding the Purpose

Business reports serve a range of purposes:

- **Information Dissemination:** Conveying facts, data, and findings to relevant stakeholders.
- **Analysis and Evaluation:** Assessing the performance of a project, strategy, or department.
- **Problem-Solving:** Identifying challenges and proposing solutions.
- **Recommendations:** Providing informed suggestions for action.

6.4.3 Structuring Your Report

A well-structured report ensures that your information is organized logically and presented coherently. It should include the following elements:

- **Title Page:** Include the report title, your name, the date, and any other pertinent information.

- **Table of Contents:** List the major sections and their corresponding page numbers.

- **Executive Summary:** Summarize the report's key points, findings, and recommendations in a concise manner.

- **Introduction:** Provide background information, objectives, and an overview of the report's content.

- **Methodology:** Explain the research methods and data collection techniques used.

- **Findings:** Present your findings in a clear and structured manner. Use visuals like charts, graphs, and tables to enhance clarity.

- **Analysis:** Interpret the findings and provide insights into the implications for the business.

- **Recommendations:** Propose actionable recommendations based on your analysis.

- **Conclusion:** Summarize the main points and reiterate the significance of your findings.

- **Appendices:** Include any supplementary material, such as raw data, supporting documents, or additional resources.

- **References:** Cite sources, references, and data used in your report.

The following is an example of business report.

Market Analysis: Consumer Preferences in the Electronics Industry

Table of Contents

1. Executive Summary
2. Introduction
3. Methodology
4. Findings
5. Analysis

---

6. Recommendations

7. Conclusion

8. References

1. Executive Summary

This report presents the results of a comprehensive market analysis conducted to understand consumer preferences within the electronics industry. The study aimed to identify trends, preferences, and factors influencing purchasing decisions.

2. Introduction

The electronics industry is rapidly evolving, with new products and technologies constantly entering the market. To remain competitive, companies need to understand consumer preferences and tailor their offerings accordingly. This report aims to provide insights into the factors that drive consumer choices in this dynamic sector.

3. Methodology

The research involved a combination of quantitative and qualitative methods. A survey was administered to a sample of 1,000 consumers, and in-depth interviews were conducted with industry experts. The data collected was analyzed using statistical techniques and thematic analysis.

4. Findings

- 75% of respondents consider product quality as the most important factor influencing their purchase decisions.
- 60% of consumers prioritize brand reputation when choosing electronics.
- 45% of participants indicated that product features and functionality are critical considerations.
- Online reviews and recommendations from friends and family influence the decisions of 80% of respondents.

5. Analysis

The findings highlight the significance of quality and reputation in the electronics industry. Consumers are increasingly relying on peer recommendations and online reviews to guide their choices. While price remains a consideration, it is secondary to factors like quality and brand image.

6. Recommendations

Based on the analysis, we recommend that companies focus on:

- Continuously improving product quality and reliability;
- Enhancing brand reputation through transparent communication and exceptional

customer service;

- Leveraging online platforms to engage with customers and showcase positive reviews;

- Incorporating consumer feedback to develop innovative features that align with their preferences.

7. Conclusion

Consumer preferences within the electronics industry are heavily influenced by product quality, brand reputation, and online reviews. Understanding these factors and adapting strategies accordingly will enable companies to attract and retain customers in this competitive landscape.

8. References

[List of sources and references consulted during the research.]

This report provides valuable insights into the electronics industry's consumer preferences. By aligning their strategies with these findings, companies can position themselves for success in an evolving market.

[Your Name]

[Your Title]

[Your Company Name]

[Date]

6.4.4 Tone and Language

Maintain a professional and objective tone in your business reports. You should follow the principles of:

- **Clarity:** Use clear and concise language to ensure the report is easily understood.

- **Objectivity:** Present information impartially and avoid personal biases.

- **Precision:** Be accurate in your language and avoid vague terms.

6.4.5 Visual Elements

Incorporate visual elements strategically to enhance the understanding and engagement of your business reports.

- **Charts and Graphs:** Use visuals to illustrate data trends and comparisons effectively.

- **Tables:** Organize complex data in tables for easy reference.

- **Visual Aids:** Include images, diagrams, or illustrations when necessary to clarify concepts.

The following is an example of business report about market analysis.

Effectiveness Analysis of IOMA Skincare Product Marketing Campaign

Table of Contents

1. Executive Summary
2. Introduction
3. Methodology
4. Findings
5. Analysis
6. Recommendations
7. Conclusion
8. References

1. Executive Summary

This report presents the results of an analysis conducted to assess the effectiveness of the recent marketing campaign for IOMA's skincare product. The campaign aimed to promote the benefits of the new skincare line and increase brand awareness among the target audience. The analysis includes findings, impact evaluation, and recommendations for enhancing future marketing efforts.

2. Introduction

The skincare industry is highly competitive, with consumers seeking products that offer visible and lasting results. IOMA introduced a new skincare product line, and a marketing campaign was launched to communicate its unique features and benefits. This report evaluates the campaign's performance in achieving its goals and resonating with the target audience.

3. Methodology

A combination of quantitative and qualitative methods was employed for this analysis. Consumer surveys were conducted to measure brand awareness, campaign recall, and product perception. Social media engagement metrics, website traffic, and sales data were also collected and analyzed. Interviews with marketing personnel provided insights into the campaign's strategy and execution.

4. Findings

- Brand Awareness: 65% of surveyed participants were aware of the IOMA skincare product line after the campaign.

- Campaign Recall: 40% of respondents recalled seeing or hearing about the campaign across various channels.
- Product Perception: Among those who recalled the campaign, 75% expressed interest in trying the skincare product.
- Engagement Metrics: Social media posts related to the campaign received 20% higher engagement compared with previous posts.
- Website Traffic: The campaign led to a 30% increase in website visits during the campaign period.
- Sales Impact: The campaign contributed to a 15% increase in sales of the promoted skincare product.

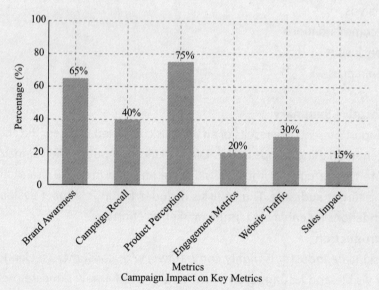

Metrics
Campaign Impact on Key Metrics

5. Analysis

The findings indicate that the marketing campaign effectively increased brand awareness, captured consumer attention, and positively influenced product perception. The higher engagement on social media and increased website traffic reflect the campaign's success in driving consumer interest.

6. Recommendations

To further improve future marketing campaigns:

- Enhancing Personalization: Tailor content to specific consumer segments to strengthen engagement and relevance.
- Strengthening Call-to-Action: Clearly communicate the next steps for consumers to take, such as visiting the website or making a purchase.

- Utilizing Influencers: Collaborate with skincare influencers to amplify the campaign's reach and credibility.
- Monitoring Feedback: Collect and analyze customer feedback to fine-tune messaging and address potential concerns.

7. Conclusion

The marketing campaign for IOMA's skincare product demonstrated its effectiveness in increasing brand awareness, engagement, and product sales. By implementing the recommendations provided, future campaigns can build on this success and foster even stronger connections with the target audience.

8. References

[List of sources and references consulted during the analysis.]

This report provides valuable insights into the impact of the recent marketing campaign and offers actionable recommendations to enhance future marketing endeavors for IOMA's skincare products.

[Your Name]

[Your Title]

[Your Company Name]

[Date]

Class Activity 5: *Write a business report analyzing the effectiveness of a recent marketing campaign. The report should present findings, analyze the campaign's impact, and provide recommendations for improvement.*

6.5
Writing Proposals

Proposals play a crucial role in business, serving as formal requests or offers that present solutions to specific problems or opportunities. Whether you're seeking funding, pitching a project, or proposing a partnership, writing a compelling and persuasive proposal is essential for achieving your goals. This section will guide you through the process of crafting effective proposals that capture the attention of your audience and demonstrate the value of your ideas.

Class Activity 6: *Figure out the significance of the following real-life business proposals.*

1. **Real Estate Industry**

   Scenario: A real estate developer wants to secure funding for a new housing project in a prime location.

   Business Proposal's Role: The developer creates a detailed proposal that outlines the project's scope, budget, expected returns, and market analysis.

2. **Technology Sector**

   Scenario: A tech start-up seeks a partnership with an established technology company to enhance its product.

   Business Proposal's Role: The start-up creates a partnership proposal that outlines its innovative technology, the benefits of collaboration, and how it aligns with the larger company's goals.

3. **Healthcare Industry**

   Scenario: A medical equipment manufacturer aims to supply a hospital with state-of-the-art equipment.

   Business Proposal's Role: The manufacturer submits a detailed proposal outlining the advantages of their equipment, its cost-effectiveness, warranty, and potential impact on patient care.

4. **Consulting Services**

   Scenario: A management consulting firm bids for a project to help a company improve its operational efficiency.

   Business Proposal's Role: The consulting firm submits a proposal that includes a problem statement, proposed solutions, a timeline, and the expected outcomes.

5. **Non-profit Sector**

   Scenario: A non-profit organization seeks funding from a foundation to support an education program for underprivileged youth.

   Business Proposal's Role: The non-profit organization crafts a grant proposal that outlines the program's objectives, budget, expected impact, and alignment with the foundation's mission.

6.5.1 Understanding the Purpose

Proposals serve different purposes, including:

- **Requesting for Funding:** Seeking financial support for projects, initiatives, or business expansions.

- **Acquiring a Project:** Presenting a plan or idea to solve a problem, seize an opportunity, or achieve a goal.

- **Requesting for Partnership:** Proposing collaboration or partnerships with other businesses or organizations.

- **Promoting Sales:** Outlining products, services, or solutions to potential clients to win contracts or projects.

The following proposal is an example of collaboration.

Bridging AI Innovation with Jiangxi University of Technology

Table of Contents

1. Executive Summary
2. Introduction
3. Objectives and Goals
4. Benefits of Collaboration
5. Proposed Collaboration Framework
6. Methodology
7. Resource Allocation
8. Expected Outcomes
9. Conclusion
10. Appendices

1. Executive Summary

We present a proposal to establish a collaborative partnership between Jiangxi University of Technology and [Advanced AI Company Name]. This collaboration aims to leverage our expertise in education and research with the cutting-edge AI capabilities of [Advanced AI Company Name] to advance AI education, research, and applications.

2. Introduction

Jiangxi University of Technology is renowned for its commitment to education, research, and innovation. With the rapid evolution of artificial intelligence, this collaboration seeks to bridge the gap between academia and industry, fostering innovation and shaping the future of AI-driven solutions.

3. Objectives and Goals

The primary objectives of this collaboration are to:

- Enhancing AI education by integrating real-world applications and industry insights;
- Facilitating collaborative research projects that address significant AI challenges;
- Promoting AI awareness and engagement within the academic community.

4. Benefits of Collaboration

Collaborating with [Advanced AI Company Name] offers several benefits, including:

- Access to advanced AI technologies, tools, and platforms;
- Opportunities for students and faculty to engage in real-world AI projects;
- Exposure to industry's best practices and latest trends;
- Contribution to the advancement of AI research and applications.

5. Proposed Collaboration Framework

The collaboration will involve:

- Jointly designing AI-focused curricula, workshops, and training programs;
- Collaborating on research projects, addressing challenges across various AI domains;
- Organizing joint seminars, conferences, and hackathons to foster AI innovation.

6. Methodology

We will establish a collaborative committee comprising representatives from Jiangxi University of Technology and [Advanced AI Company Name]. This committee will oversee the development and execution of collaborative initiatives, ensuring alignment with the partnership's goals.

7. Resource Allocation

To facilitate this collaboration, we propose allocating resources for:

- Curriculum development and integration;
- Research project support, including funding and resources;
- Organizing events, workshops, and seminars.

8. Expected Outcomes

We anticipate that this collaboration will lead to:

- Enriched AI education that prepares students for industry demands;
- Collaborative research outputs that contribute to AI advancements;
- Elevated AI awareness and engagement within the academic community.

9. Conclusion

By forging a partnership with [Advanced AI Company Name], Jiangxi University of Technology aims to create a dynamic ecosystem that nurtures AI talent, drives innovation, and pushes the boundaries of AI applications. We believe that this collaboration will not only benefit our institutions but also contribute significantly to the AI landscape.

10. Appendices

[Profiles of key individuals involved in the collaboration]

[Letters of support or interest from relevant departments]

[List of potential collaborative projects]

Thank you for considering this proposal. We are excited about the opportunity to collaborate with [Advanced AI Company Name] and look forward to jointly shaping the future of AI education and research.

Sincerely,

[Your Name]

[Your Title]

[Your School Name]

[Your Contact Information]

[Date]

6.5.2　Structuring Your Proposal

A well-structured proposal ensures clarity and persuasiveness. It should include the following elements:

- **Title Page:** Include the proposal title, your name, the date, and the recipient's information.

- **Table of Contents:** List the major sections and their corresponding page numbers.

- **Executive Summary:** Summarize the main points, benefits, and objectives of the proposal.

- **Problem Statement:** Clearly define the problem or opportunity you're addressing.

- **Objectives and Goals:** State the desired outcomes of your proposal.

- **Solution or Approach:** Describe your proposed solution, product, service, or project plan.

- **Methodology:** Outline the steps you'll take to implement your proposal.

- **Budget and Costs:** Present a detailed breakdown of the budget, including expenses and potential returns.

- **Timeline:** Provide a timeline for project implementation or expected results.

- **Benefits and Value:** Explain the benefits and value your proposal offers to the recipient.

- **Conclusion:** Summarize the key points and reiterate the benefits of your proposal.

- **Appendices:** Include additional supporting materials, such as references, relevant research, and data.

The following proposal is an example of funding.

Empowering Expecting Parents: A Comprehensive Support Program for Pregnant Individuals

Table of Contents

1. Executive Summary
2. Introduction
3. Problem Statement
4. Objectives and Goals
5. Proposed Solution
6. Methodology
7. Budget and Funding Request
8. Benefits and Impact
9. Conclusion
10. Appendices

1. Executive Summary

We present a proposal to establish a comprehensive support program for pregnant individuals, aimed at providing essential resources, guidance, and care during their pregnancy journey. This initiative seeks funding to ensure that every pregnant person receives the necessary support to foster healthy pregnancies and ensure positive outcomes for both parents and newborns.

2. Introduction

Pregnancy is a transformative period that demands physical, emotional, and financial support. However, many pregnant individuals lack access to adequate resources and information. Our proposed program aims to bridge this gap by offering holistic support to expecting parents.

3. Problem Statement

Pregnant individuals often face challenges such as limited access to prenatal care, financial strain, and lack of educational resources. These issues can adversely impact maternal and fetal health, leading to a higher risk of complications.

4. Objectives and Goals

The primary objectives of the program are to:

- Ensuring access to quality prenatal care for all pregnant individuals;
- Providing educational resources to empower individuals to make informed decisions during pregnancy;
- Alleviating financial burdens through targeted assistance.

5. Proposed Solution

The comprehensive support program will include:

- Access to free or affordable prenatal medical check-ups and consultations;
- Educational workshops on prenatal care, childbirth, and newborn care;
- Financial assistance for essential pregnancy-related expenses, such as healthcare costs and maternity clothing.

6. Methodology

We will collaborate with local healthcare providers, educators, and community organizations to deliver the program's components. Workshops and medical services will be organized in accessible community spaces, ensuring inclusivity.

7. Budget and Funding Request

To successfully implement this program, we seek funding in the amount of [Total Funding Amount]. This funding will cover medical services, educational materials, workshop facilitators, administrative costs, and financial assistance for eligible participants.

8. Benefits and Impact

The proposed program will have a positive impact on:

- Maternal and fetal health outcomes;
- Overall pregnancy experience for individuals and families;
- Reducing financial stress associated with pregnancy.

9. Conclusion

By supporting this program, we aim to contribute to healthier pregnancies and improved birth outcomes, ultimately benefiting both individuals and their communities. We believe that investing in the well-being of pregnant individuals aligns with our collective commitment to fostering healthy families and a strong society.

10. Appendices

[List of supporting documents, including research studies and partner agreements.]

Thank you for considering our proposal to fund this vital initiative. Your support will directly contribute to the well-being of pregnant individuals and the creation of a supportive and inclusive community.

Sincerely,

[Your Name]

[Your Title]

[Your Contact Information]

[Date]

6.5.3 Tone and Language

Maintain a persuasive and professional tone in your proposals. You should follow the principles of:

- **Clarity:** Clearly present your ideas and solutions, avoiding jargon or unnecessary complexity.

- **Persuasiveness:** Use persuasive language to convince the recipient of the value of your proposals.

- **Confidence:** Display confidence in your proposals' feasibility and benefits.

6.5.4 Visual Elements

Incorporate visual elements to enhance the presentation and understanding of your proposals.

- **Graphs and Charts:** Use visuals to illustrate data, trends, or projected outcomes.

- **Images:** Include relevant images or diagrams to provide clarity.

- **Formatting:** Use headings, bullet points, and lists to improve readability.

Class Activity 7: *Write a proposal outlining a new product's launch strategy for a cosmetic company. The proposal should include the details such as target audience, marketing channels, and expected outcomes. You may fulfill the proposal according to the template below.*

Elevate Beauty with Mary Cohe Cosmetics

Table of Contents

1. Executive Summary

2. Introduction

3. Objectives and Goals

4. Target Audience

5. Marketing Channels

6. Product Features and Benefits

7. Promotion and Outreach Plan

8. Expected Outcomes

9. Conclusion

10. Appendices

1. Executive Summary

We present a comprehensive proposal for the launch of an exciting new product under Mary Cohe Cosmetics. This proposal outlines:

_____

_____

2. Introduction

Mary Cohe Cosmetics has a rich legacy of delivering high-quality beauty products. This proposal

_____

_____

3. Objectives and Goals

The primary objectives of this product launch strategy are to:

_____

_____

4. Target Audience

The new product is designed to appeal to:

_____

_____

5. Marketing Channels

To effectively reach our target audience, we will utilize a multi-channel approach, including:

_____

_____

_____

6. Product Features and Benefits

The new product offers:

_____

_____

_____

7. Promotion and Outreach Plan

Our promotion plan includes:

_____

_____

_____

8. Expected Outcomes

We anticipate the following outcomes from this product's launch strategy:

_____

_____

_____

9. Conclusion

_____

_____

_____

10. Appendices

_____

_____

[Product images and mock-ups]

[Sample social media content calendar]

[Influencer collaboration proposals]

Thank you for considering this proposal. We look forward to implementing this strategy and achieving remarkable success with the launch of our new product.

Sincerely,

[Your Name]

[Your Title]

Mary Cohe Cosmetics

[Your Contact Information]

[Date]

Class Activity 8: *Choose one of the following hypothetical proposal scenarios and write a business proposal.*

1. **Start-up Funding Proposal**

   You have a brilliant tech start-up idea and need funding to bring it to life. Write a proposal to pitch your start-up to potential investors, explaining your concept, market potential, and the expected return on investment.

2. **Marketing Campaign Proposal**

   You work for a marketing agency, and a client wants to launch a new product. Write a proposal outlining your marketing strategy, including target audience analysis, campaign ideas, budget, and expected outcomes.

3. **Project Management Proposal**

   Your company is bidding for a government project. Write a proposal that outlines your project management approach, team expertise, timeline, and budget.

4. **Product Development Proposal**

   You work for a manufacturing company, and your team has an idea for a new product. Write a proposal to present your product concept, market research, production plan, and projected revenue.

5. **Research Project Proposal**

   You are a researcher in a university, and you want to conduct a study on a pressing social issue. Write a proposal to request funding from a research grant organization, explaining the significance of the study, your research methods, and expected contributions to the field.

Unit 7

Special Topics

In the dynamic landscape of business communication, certain contexts demand specialized approaches to effectively conveying your message and achieve your goals. This unit delves into how to write specific business contexts, each requiring its own unique strategies and techniques. From job hunting to social media, public relations, and marketing, this unit will explore how to tailor your communication to suit the demands of various specialized scenarios.

7.1
Writing for Job Hunting

In the landscape of professional opportunities, your resumé acts as a key to unlocking potential job interviews. It is more than a mere summary of your history; it's a strategic tool to market your greatest asset—yourself. This section will guide you through the art and science of crafting a resumé that not only outlines your qualifications but also contains the essence of your professional persona.

7.1.1 Resumé Writing

A resumé serves as a snapshot of your professional journey, highlighting your skills, experiences, and achievements. Its purpose is to garner the interest of employers and secure a job interview. We'll explore the different purposes resumés serve in various stages of your career and how to adapt them to your current professional needs.

1. Understanding the Purpose of a Resumé

1) Securing an Interview

A resumé's foremost objective is to land you an interview. It's not meant to be a comprehensive work history but a summary highlighting why you're the right fit for a specific role.

Suppose you're a marketing specialist applying for a digital marketing role. Your resumé should focus on specific digital marketing campaigns you've managed, showcasing your skills in this area rather than detailing every job you've ever had.

2) Highlighting Professional Skills and Achievements

Your resumé should highlight the skills that are most relevant to the job you're applying for. For a project manager role, you should emphasize leadership, organizational capability, and problem-solving skills by detailing the projects you've made.

Rather than just listing duties, your resumé should focus on what you've accomplished in your roles. If you increased sales by 20% in your previous job, don't just say "Responsible for sales". Instead, write "Increased sales by 20% through targeted customer engagement strategies".

3) Tailoring to the Job

Customize your resumé to echo the language and requirements of the job description. If the job requires "excellent customer service skills", you can provide examples from the past roles where you demonstrated these skills.

4) Creating a Professional Narrative

Your resumé should weave a narrative that connects your past experiences to your future aspirations. If you're moving from a sales role to a marketing role, highlight how your sales experience provided you with unique insights into customer behavior, which will be beneficial in a marketing context.

5) Conveying Personal Branding

Your resumé should reflect your personal brand—what makes you unique and a great fit for the company's culture. Use a tone and language in your resumé that aligns with the company's culture, whether it's formal, innovative, or collaborative.

By understanding these aspects, you can craft a resumé that not only just lists your past jobs and duties, but also effectively communicates your value, aligns with your career goals, and resonates with potential employers. This approach ensures your resumé serves as a powerful tool in your job search journey.

2.　Components of an Effective Resumé

A well-crafted resumé comprises several key components, each serving a specific purpose. The key elements include contact information, summary statement, work experience, education, skills, and additional sections like certifications or volunteer work. We'll provide insights into what recruiters look for in each section and how to present your information in a clear, concise, and engaging manner.

1) Contact Information

This section should include your name, phone number, e-mail address, and LinkedIn profile (if applicable). For example:

John Doe
Phone: (123) 456-7890
E-mail: john.doe@e-mail.com
LinkedIn: linkedin.com/in/johndoe

Recruiter Insight: Ensure your contact information is updated and professional. Avoid quirky e-mail addresses; use one that's simple and based on your name.

2) Summary Statement

This section means to provide a brief overview of your professional background, key skills, and what you're seeking in your next role. For example:

Experienced digital marketing specialist with a track record of increasing online engagement by over 30%. Seeking to leverage my expertise in a dynamic marketing team.

Recruiter Insight: Tailor this to the job you're applying for, incorporating keywords from the job description.

3) Work Experience

Structure: List your work history in reverse chronological order. Your work experience should include job title, company name, dates of employment, and a brief description of your responsibilities and achievements. For example:

Digital Marketing Manager
ABC Corp, Jan. 2018–Present

- Led a team of 5 to implement digital marketing strategies, resulting in a 40% increase in web traffic.
- Managed a budget of $500K, optimizing ad spend and increasing ROI by 25%.

Recruiter Insight: Focus on achievements and outcomes, not just duties. Use quantifiable results where possible.

4) Education

Details: List your highest educational attainment, including the degree, institution, and graduation year. For example:

Bachelor of Science in Marketing
University of XYZ, May 2016

Recruiter Insight: If you're a recent graduate, you may include relevant coursework or academic achievements. For more experienced professionals, keep this section brief.

5) Skills

Listing: Include a mix of hard and soft skills relevant to the job. For example:

- Hard Skills: SEO, Google Analytics, CRM Software
- Soft Skills: Leadership, Communication, Problem-solving

Recruiter Insight: Align your skills with the job requirements and avoid overgeneralizing. Be prepared to demonstrate these skills in your interviews.

6) Additional Sections

Certifications: If applicable, include any relevant certifications and showcase your community involvement and additional skills. For example:

- Certified Digital Marketing Professional (CDMP), 2019

Volunteer Work:

- Volunteer Coordinator, Local Food Bank, 2017–2018

Recruiter Insight: These sections can differentiate you from other candidates, especially if they align with the company's values or the job's requirements.

Each of these components plays a vital role in creating a comprehensive picture of your professional qualifications. Remember, the key is to present your information in a way that is not only clear and concise but also compelling and tailored to the role you're aiming for.

Sample Resumé for an Undergraduate Business English Student

Wenbo ZHANG

99 Ziyang Road

Nanchang, China, 330022

1331××××966

Wenbo-Zhang@163.com

LinkedIn: [Your LinkedIn Profile]

Objective

Enthusiastic and dedicated Business English undergraduate with a strong interest in corporate communication and international business relations. Seeking an internship position to apply my language skills and business knowledge in a real-world environment.

Education

Bachelor of Arts in Business English

Jiangxi Normal University, Nanchang, Jiangxi, China

Expected Graduation: July, 2026

Key Courses: International Business Communication, Business Writing, Marketing Principles, Cross-Cultural Management

Relevant Skills

Communication Skills: Proficient in crafting clear, persuasive written and verbal communication.

Research and Analysis: Able to conduct thorough research and analyze data to inform business decisions.

Team Collaboration: Experienced in working effectively in team settings, both as a leader and a contributor.

Language Skills: Fluent in English and [other language if applicable]; basic proficiency in [additional language if applicable].

Academic Projects

Market Analysis Project | [Course Name], [University], [Semester and Year]

- Conducted comprehensive market research and analysis on [topic/industry].
- Presented findings to class, highlighting key trends and potential business strategies.

Cross-Cultural Communication Presentation | [Course Name], [University], [Semester and Year]

- Developed and delivered a presentation on effective communication strategies in international business contexts.
- Focused on cultural sensitivity, language nuances, and non-verbal communication.

Internship Experience

Business Development Intern | [Company Name], [City, Country] [Month, Year]—[Month, Year]

- Assisted in developing and implementing business strategies to attract new clients.
- Supported market research efforts to identify and analyze potential business opportunities.
- Collaborated with the marketing team to create promotional materials.

Volunteer Experience

Event Coordinator, [Event/Charity Name], [City, Country] [Month, Year]—Present

- Organized and coordinated events aimed at [purpose of even ts].
- Managed a team of volunteers, demonstrating leadership and organizational skills.

Certifications

[Relevant Certification Name], [Issuing Organization], [Year if recent]

Languages

English (Native)

[Other Language] (Fluent)

[Additional Language] (Basic)

Interests

Global economics, public speaking, content creation, travel and cultural exploration

The sample above is designed to give you an idea of how to present your academic and extracurricular experiences effectively. Tailor your resumé to reflect your unique experiences, skills, and interests. Remember, clarity, brevity, and relevance to the job you are applying for are key to a successful resumé.

Sample Resumé for an Experienced Job Hunter

[Your Name]

[Your Address]

[City, State, Zip]

[Your Phone Number]

[Your Professional E-mail Address]

LinkedIn: [Your LinkedIn Profile]

Professional Summary

Accomplished and bilingual professional with extensive experience in interpretation and language services, seeking to leverage language skills and cross-cultural communication expertise in a new career path. Adaptability, strong analytical skills, and a passion for continuous learning, aiming to transition into a role where these competencies can be applied in a business or technology environment.

Professional Experience

Senior Interpreter [Company Name], [City, Country] [Month, Year]–Present

• Provided high-quality interpretation services for a range of corporate and governmental clients, ensuring accurate and culturally sensitive communication.

  • Led a team of interpreters, managing scheduling, training, and quality assurance.

  • Collaborated with international teams, facilitating effective communication across language barriers in high-stakes meetings and negotiations.

  • Implemented new technology solutions to enhance efficiency and accuracy in interpretation services.

Interpreter and Translator [Company Name], [City, Country] [Month, Year]–[Month, Year]

  • Performed simultaneous and consecutive interpretation for various events, including conferences, seminars, and business meetings.

  • Translated complex documents, maintaining the integrity and meaning of the original text.

  • Assisted in the development of training materials for new interpreters, focusing on industry-specific terminology and cultural nuances.

Career Transition Objective

Seeking to apply my extensive language expertise and cross-cultural communication skills in a new role that embraces technological advancements. Interested in opportunities in business development, international relations, or technology sectors, where I can contribute to a team navigating global markets and multicultural environments.

Education

Bachelor of Arts in Linguistics

[University Name], [City, Country]

Graduated [Month, Year]

Skills

Expertise in English and [other language]

Proficient in cross-cultural communication and negotiation

Strong analytical and problem-solving abilities

Adaptability to new technologies and industries

Team leadership and training experience

Certifications and Professional Development

Certified Interpreter, [Certification Body], [Year]

Completed course in Business Management, [Institute or Platform], [Year]

Ongoing training in emerging AI technologies and applications

Languages

English (Native)

[Other Language] (Fluent)

[Additional Language] (Intermediate)

Interests

Technology trends, artificial intelligence in business, global economics, cultural exchange programs

The above resumé is tailored to showcase how your skills as an interpreter can be relevant in different sectors, especially those embracing AI and technological advancements. Highlighting your adaptability, language skills, and willingness to engage with new technologies makes you a strong candidate for roles beyond traditional interpreting. Tailor this template to reflect your own experiences and the specific requirements of the roles you are targeting.

3. Tailoring Your Resumé to Job Descriptions

One size does not fit all when it comes to resumés. Tailoring your resumé to specific job descriptions can significantly increase your chances of landing an interview. The following section will teach you how to analyze job postings and identify keywords and skills to highlight in your resumé, ensuring it resonates with the specific requirements and expectations of your potential employers.

Customizing your resumé for each job application is crucial for standing out among other candidates. This process involves carefully analyzing the job description and aligning your resumé to match its requirements. Here's a detailed approach with examples.

1) Analyzing Job Postings

Identify Keywords: Look for specific skills, experiences, and qualifications mentioned in the job description. If the job posting emphasizes "project management", "team leadership", and "effective communication", these are the keywords you should incorporate into your resumé.

Understand the Role: Grasp the primary responsibilities and what the employer values most in a candidate. For a marketing role that focuses on digital channels, highlight your experience with digital marketing tools and strategies.

2) Matching Your Experience and Skills

Highlight Relevant Experience: Align your past job responsibilities and achievements with the ones listed in the job description. If the job requires experience in "managing a sales team", detail your experience in a previous role where you led a sales team to achieve specific targets.

Showcase Relevant Skills: If the job description emphasizes certain skills, make sure these are clearly mentioned in your resumé. For a job that requires proficiency in a specific software, include this in your skills section and mention any relevant projects where you used this tool.

3) Customizing the Summary and Objective

Tailor Your Summary/Objective: Modify your resumé's summary or objective to reflect the specific role you're applying for. If you apply for a customer service manager position, your summary should highlight your experience in customer service and team management.

Incorporating Keywords: Incorporate the language and phrasing from the job description into your resumé. If the job description mentions "excellent organizational skills", use the same phrase in your resumé.

4) Providing Quantifiable Evidence

Use Numbers and Results: Where possible, use numbers to quantify your achievements and align them with the job requirements. If applying for a sales position, mention something like, "Increased sales by 20% over a 12-month period through strategic client engagement."

5) Adapting the Resumé Layout

Prioritize Relevant Information: Arrange your resumé sections to highlight the most relevant experience and skills at the top. If applying for a technical role, place your technical skills and related project experiences near the top of your resumé. The following is an example of tailoring a resumé:

Before tailoring:

Work Experience: Listed in chronological order, starting with the most recent job.

Skills: A general list of skills including teamwork, communication, and problem-solving.

Work Experience:

Job 1: Sales Associate at Company A, 2020–Present
- Assisted customers in finding products.
- Managed inventory levels.

Job 2: Customer Service Representative at Company B, 2018–2020
- Answered customer inquiries via phone and e-mail.
- Resolved complaints and ensured customer satisfaction.

Skills:

Teamwork

Communication

Problem-Solving

Microsoft Office Suite

After tailoring for a project manager position:

Work Experience: Highlighted project management roles and specific achievements related to successful project completion.

Skills: Included specific skills like Agile methodologies, budget management, and stakeholder communication, as mentioned in the job description.

Work Experience:

Job 1: Project Coordinator at Company C, 2021–Present
- Led a team of 5 in developing and implementing a new inventory tracking system that reduced product loss by 20%.
- Managed project timeline and budget, ensuring project completion 3 weeks ahead of schedule and under budget by 10%.

Job 2: Assistant Project Manager at Company D, 2019–2021
- Assisted in managing a large-scale software development project, applying Agile methodologies to improve team efficiency.
- Facilitated stakeholder communication, presenting monthly progress reports to clients and gathering feedback to adjust project scope and timelines.

Skills:
- Agile and Scrum methodologies
- Budget management and cost control
- Stakeholder communication and engagement
- Risk assessment and mitigation strategies
- Proficient in Microsoft Project and JIRA

Remember, the goal of tailoring your resumé is to make it as relevant as possible to the job you're applying for. This not only shows that you're a good fit for the position but also demonstrates your attention to details and your genuine interest in the role.

Class Activity 1: *Work in groups to tailor the generic resumé to each job description below.*

Generic Resumé:

Objective: Enthusiastic professional seeking to leverage diverse experience in a dynamic new role. Excel in teamwork, communication, and problem-solving.

Work Experience:

Business Analyst, XYZ Corp, 2019–2021
- Analyzed business processes and recommended improvements.
- Facilitated communication between IT and other departments.

Associate, ABC Inc., 2017–2019
- Supported project teams and managed documentation.
- Assisted in client meetings and presentations.

Skills:
- Communication
- Teamwork
- Problem-Solving
- Microsoft Office Suite

Job Descriptions

A. Software Engineer

Responsibilities: Develop and maintain software applications, collaborate with cross-functional teams to define specifications, and troubleshoot code issues.

Required Skills: Proficiency in programming languages (e.g., Python, Java), experience with software development life cycle (SDLC), and knowledge of database management.

B. Digital Marketing Specialist

Responsibilities: Develop digital marketing campaigns, analyze web traffic, and manage social media presence to increase brand awareness.

Required Skills: SEO/SEM, content creation, social media management, and analytical skills.

C. Financial Analyst

Responsibilities: Analyze financial data, prepare reports for management, and recommend investment opportunities.

Required Skills: Financial modeling, data analysis, proficiency in Excel, and understanding of financial markets.

D. Project Manager

Responsibilities: Oversee project execution, manage budgets and timelines, and ensure the successful completion of projects.

Required Skills: Leadership, budget management, risk management, and familiarity with project management software.

E. Human Resources Manager

Responsibilities: Manage recruitment processes, develop HR policies, and oversee employee relations.

Required Skills: Communication, conflict resolution, employment law knowledge, and experience with HR software.

F. Sales Manager

Responsibilities: Drive sales team performance, develop sales strategies, and manage client relationships.

Required Skills: Sales strategy, customer relationship management (CRM) software, negotiation, and team leadership.

G. Graphic Designer

Responsibilities: Create visual concepts, design graphics for various media, and collaborate with teams to meet marketing needs.

Required Skills: Proficiency in design software (e.g., Adobe Creative Suite), creativity, and understanding of branding.

H. Supply Chain Analyst

Responsibilities: Analyze supply chain operations, recommend improvements for efficiency, and manage inventory levels.

Required Skills: Data analysis, logistics knowledge, proficiency in supply chain management software, and problem-solving.

4. Resumé Formatting and Design

The visual appeal of your resumé is crucial. It's the first thing recruiters notice, even before they read a single word. The following will discuss various formatting styles (chronological, functional, and combination) and the importance of a clean, professional layout. Tips on font choice, spacing, and color schemes will be provided to help your resumé stand out while maintaining a professional look.

1) Choosing a Resumé Format

Chronological Format: work experiences in reverse chronological order, which is the best for those with a solid work history in the same field as the job they're applying for. If you've been working in marketing for the last 10 years, list your jobs starting with the most recent and work backward.

Functional Format: Focus on skills and experiences, rather than work history, which is suitable for career changers or those with gaps in employment. If you want to transition from teaching to content writing, emphasize skills like communication, curriculum development, and editing, rather than focusing on the chronological order of jobs.

Combination Format: Blend the chronological and functional formats. Highlight skills while providing a timeline of work history. For someone with experience in both sales and management, list key skills in sales and management at the top, followed by a chronological list of jobs.

Class Activity 2: *Identify the resumé format in the following three resumés.*

Resumé 1

John Doe

Objective: Experienced marketing professional seeking a senior position to leverage my expertise in campaign management and strategic planning.

Work Experience

Marketing Manager, ABC Corporation (2018–Present)

- Led a team of 10 marketing specialists to develop and implement comprehensive marketing strategies.
- Increased company sales by 25% through targeted online advertising campaigns.

Marketing Coordinator, XYZ Inc. (2015–2018)

- Coordinated marketing projects from conception to completion.
- Assisted with the development of marketing materials and social media content.

Education

Bachelor of Science in Marketing, University of City, 2015

Skills

- Strategic planning
- Team leadership
- Digital marketing

Resumé 2

Jane Smith

Objective: Creative graphic designer with a passion for innovative design solutions seeking a challenging role.

Skills and Accomplishments

Graphic Design: Created compelling designs for print and digital media for over 50 clients. Proficient in Adobe Creative Suite.

Project Management: Managed multiple design projects simultaneously, ensuring timely delivery and client satisfaction.

Creativity: Developed a branding package for a start-up that increased their market visibility by 30%.

Work Experience

Freelance Graphic Designer, Self-employed (2016–Present)

Junior Graphic Designer, Creative Studio (2014–2016)

Education

Bachelor of Fine Arts in Graphic Design, Design Institute, 2014

Resumé 3

Alex Johnson

Objective: Seasoned project manager aiming to leverage extensive background in project execution and team management in a dynamic new environment.

Skills and Accomplishments

Project Management: Successfully managed over 30 large-scale projects, leading to a 40% increase in efficiency.

Leadership: Directed teams of up to 20 members, fostering a collaborative and productive work environment.

Budget Management: Oversaw project budgets of up to $2 million, reducing costs by 15% without compromising on quality.

Professional Experience

Senior Project Manager, DEF Solutions (2017–Present)

Spearheaded the development and delivery of technology solutions, resulting in a 50% increase in customer satisfaction.

Project Coordinator, GHI Technologies (2014–2017)

Assisted in the management of project schedules and resources, ensuring projects were delivered on time and within budget.

Education

Master of Business Administration, University of City, 2017

Bachelor of Science in Computer Science, State College, 2014

2) Layout and Design Elements

Clear and Professional Layout: Use a clear, organized layout with distinct headings and adequate spacing. For example, use bold headings for sections like "Experience", "Education", and "Skills", and make sure there's enough white space between lines and sections.

Font Choice: Choose a professional and easy-to-read font. Fonts like Arial, Calibri, or Times New Roman in size 10–12 points are typically good choices.

Color Scheme: Use color sparingly and professionally. Remember, stick to one or two colors besides black. For instance, use a dark blue for headings and black for body text.

Consistent Formatting: Maintain consistency throughout your resumé in terms of font size, bullet points, and line spacing. If you use bullet points in your "Experience" section, use them in all sections where lists are present.

3) Visual Hierarchy

Emphasize Important Information: Use formatting tools like bolding or italics to highlight important details like job titles or achievements. For example, bold your job titles and the names of the companies you worked for.

4) Incorporating Margins and Spacing

Appropriate Margins: Use standard margins (typically around 1 inch) to ensure your resumé looks balanced. Don't reduce margins so much that your resumé looks crowded. Keep enough white space for readability.

5) Use of Graphics and Icons

Use graphics and icons only if they add value and are relevant to your field. For example, a graphic designer might use a small, tasteful graphic to display proficiency in different design software. The following is an example of a well-formatted resumé:

Header: "John Doe" in bold, slightly larger font. Contact information directly below in a smaller font.

Professional Summary: A brief section providing an overview of qualifications.

Experience: Each job title in bold, company name, and dates of employment in regular font, and bullet points for achievements and responsibilities.

Education: University name and degree in bold, and graduation date in regular font.

Skills: Listed in two columns with bullet points, using a slightly smaller font.

The following is an example.

John Doe
123 Main Street | City, State 12345 | (123) 456-7890 | e-mail@example.com

Professional Summary
A dynamic and creative graphic designer with 5 years of experience in creating

---

compelling visuals for digital and print media. Proficient in Adobe Creative Suite, with a strong ability to communicate complex ideas through design. Passionate about bringing brands to life through innovative visual storytelling.

Experience

Senior Graphic Designer, Creative Solutions Inc., City, State | May 2019–Present
- **Led the design team** in developing branding, advertising, and marketing materials that increased client engagement by 30%.
- **Collaborated with clients** to understand their vision and translated it into impactful graphic designs.
- **Managed multiple projects**, meeting tight deadlines without compromising on quality.

Graphic Designer, DesignWorks Studio, City, State | July 2015–April 2019
- **Developed visual concepts** for a range of digital and print campaigns, resulting in a 20% increase in customer acquisition.
- **Enhanced brand consistency** by standardizing the visual identity across all marketing channels.
- **Provided creative direction** for photo shoots and digital imagery, improving the aesthetic appeal of the final product.

Education

Bachelor of Fine Arts in Graphic Design, **University of the Arts,** City, State | Graduated May 2015

Skills

Adobe Photoshop	**Adobe Illustrator**
• Adobe InDesign	• Web Design
• Typography	• Brand Development
• Motion Graphics	• UI/UX Design

In conclusion, the formatting and design of your resumé play a critical role in how your information is perceived. A well-designed resumé not only attracts the recruiter's attention but also enhances the readability and impact of your content.

5. Common Mistakes and How to Avoid Them

This subsection will address common pitfalls such as typos, overloading information, using clichés, and being too vague or too detailed. It will equip you with strategies to avoid these errors, ensuring your resumé is as flawless as it is impressive.

Crafting a resumé is a delicate balance between providing enough information to pique an employer's interest and not overwhelming them with irrelevant details. Here are some common pitfalls and strategies to avoid them.

1) Typos and Grammatical Errors

Minor spelling mistakes or grammatical errors can give an impression of carelessness. So, always proofread your resumé multiple times. Use tools like WPS, or ask someone else to review it.

2) Overloading Information

Cramming too much information onto your resumé can overwhelm the employer and bury important details. Instead, be concise and include only the most relevant experience and skills. Aim for a one-page resumé, especially if you have less than 10 years of experience.

3) Using Clichés and Buzzwords

Overused phrases like "team player" or "hard worker" are vague and do not distinguish you. You can use specific examples and achievements to demonstrate your skills. For example, instead of saying "excellent communication skills", mention a successful project you led that required effective communication.

4) Being Too Vague or Too Detailed

Failing to provide enough detail can leave the employer guessing, while too much detail can dilute the impact of your key achievements. The way to avoid it is to use quantifiable achievements and be specific about your role in them, but don't delve into unnecessary minutiae. For example, instead of saying "Managed a team", specify "Managed a team of 10 sales associates, increasing department sales by 25%".

5) Inconsistent Formatting

Using various fonts, sizes, or bullet point styles can make your resumé look unprofessional. Stick to one or two fonts and be consistent with formatting throughout the document. For example, using Times New Roman for one section and Arial for another.

6) Lack of Tailoring for the Job

Sending a generic resumé to every job application is not appropriate. You are supposed to customize your resumé for each job you apply for, aligning your skills and experiences with the job description. For example, highlight your experience in social media marketing when applying for a social media manager role.

7) Incorrect Use of Tenses

Inconsistent or incorrect use of tenses throughout the resumé should be avoided. Use past tense for previous jobs and present tense for your current role.

8) Not Including Keywords from Job Description

The last one is failing to include relevant keywords found in the job description. Incorporating keywords from the job listing can make your resumé more likely to get past Applicant Tracking Systems (ATS). If the job description mentions "CRM software", include your experience with specific CRM tools in your resumé.

By avoiding these common mistakes, your resumé will present you in the best possible light, demonstrating attention to detail, relevance to the role, and a professional approach to your job search.

Class Activity 3: *Rewrite the following two versions of a resumé section to make them specific yet concise, focusing on quantifiable achievements.*

Too Vague	Too Detailed
Work Experience Marketing Specialist • Worked on marketing campaigns. • Managed social media. • Handled marketing tasks.	Work Experience Marketing Specialist at XYZ Corporation, June, 2018–August, 2021 • Was responsible for the initial conceptualization, detailed planning, execution, and post-campaign analysis of over 15 marketing campaigns, involving extensive market research, competitor analysis, budget allocation across digital and traditional channels, coordination with multiple departments (design, content, sales), adjustment and reallocation of resources based on mid-campaign performance data, and comprehensive performance reporting. • Managed the company's social media presence across seven platforms, including Facebook, Twitter, Instagram, LinkedIn, Pinterest, TikTok, and Snapchat, creating and scheduling over 3,000 posts, analyzing engagement data to optimize posting times and content

(Continued)

Too Vague	Too Detailed
	types, responding to comments and messages, and running targeted advertising campaigns with a monthly budget of up to $5,000.
	• Handled a wide array of additional marketing tasks, such as e-mail marketing campaigns (designing, sending, and analyzing over 100 campaigns), organizing and promoting five major corporate events (including venue selection, vendor management, ticket sales, and post-event feedback collection), and conducting monthly competitor analysis reports.

7.1.2 Cover Letter Writing

A cover letter is a vital document in the job application process, serving as a personal introduction and complementing your resumé. This section will explore the importance and functions of a cover letter, supported by examples and best practices.

1. Understanding the Role of a Cover Letter

A cover letter is your first opportunity to introduce yourself to a potential employer. It's where you can express your enthusiasm for the position and the company. For example:

> I am excited to apply for the marketing manager position at XYZ Corporation, a company I have long admired for its innovative approach to digital marketing.

While your resumé provides a factual summary of your skills and experiences, a cover letter allows you to elaborate on these points, providing context and personal insights. For example:

> In my previous role as a sales coordinator, I developed a new client onboarding process, enhancing client satisfaction by 25%.

As a critical component of business English writing, a cover letter demonstrates your ability to communicate effectively in writing. A well-structured, clear, and concise cover letter reflects your communication skills.

2. Common Purposes of a Cover Letter

1) Highlighting Fit for the Role and Company

The cover letter should be customized for each job application, showing how your skills and experiences align with the job requirements. For example:

> With my extensive background in team leadership and project management, I am well-prepared to contribute to the innovative projects at XYZ Corporation.

It should also demonstrate your understanding of and alignment with the company's culture, values, and mission. For example:

> I am particularly drawn to XYZ's commitment to sustainability, innovation, and values that resonate deeply with my professional ethos.

2) Addressing Gaps or Changes in Career Path

A cover letter is an ideal place to explain any career shifts or gaps in employment. For example:

> After a rewarding career in journalism, I am eager to utilize my storytelling skills in a corporate communication role.

If there's something unique in your resumé that needs clarification, the cover letter provides a chance to explain. For example:

> I took a two-year hiatus from my professional career to volunteer abroad, gaining valuable cross-cultural communication skills.

3) Making a Compelling Case for Your Candidacy

Use your cover letter to persuade the employer why you are the best candidate for the job. For example:

> My combination of creative marketing strategies and a data-driven approach to decision-making uniquely positions me to contribute effectively to your team.

End your cover letter with a call to action, expressing your eagerness to discuss your candidacy further. For example:

> I am very enthusiastic about the possibility of joining XYZ Corporation and would welcome the opportunity to discuss how my skills and experiences align with your team's current needs.

In summary, a cover letter is more than a formality; it's a powerful tool to express your interest, showcase your qualifications, and make a strong case for why you are the ideal candidate for the job.

3. Structuring Your Cover Letter

The cover letter is an integral part of your job application. It is your first opportunity to make a strong impression on a potential employer. A well-structured cover letter can set you apart from other candidates. This section will guide you through the essential components of a cover letter, ensuring it is effectively organized and impactful.

1) Header

Start with your contact information at the top. This section should include your name, address, phone number, and e-mail address. If applicable, include your LinkedIn profile. Follow this with the date, and then the employer's contact information.

2) Salutation

Address the letter to a specific person, using his or her name and title. If you cannot find a name, use a general greeting such as "Dear Hiring Manager".

3) Opening Paragraph

The opening paragraph should grab the employer's attention. Briefly introduce yourself and state the position you are applying for. Mention how you learned about the position. If you have a mutual contact or referral, mention them here.

4) Middle Paragraph(s)

This section is the core of your cover letter. Here, you should detail why you are a good fit for the job. Connect your skills and experience to the requirements listed in the job description. Use specific examples to demonstrate your achievements and how they can benefit the employer. If you have relevant statistics or figures, include them here.

5) Closing Paragraph

In the closing paragraph, reiterate your interest in the position and the company. Mention any enclosed documents, such as your resumé. Thank the employer for considering your application and express your willingness to discuss your qualifications in more detail during an interview.

6) Formal Closing

End your letter with a formal closing such as "Sincerely" or "Best regards", followed by your name. If you are submitting a hard copy, leave space for your handwritten signature above your typed name.

7) Enclosures or Attachments

If you mention any enclosures or attachments in your cover letter (like your resumé), make sure to list them after your signature.

A well-structured cover letter is a critical component of your job application. Each part has a specific purpose and contributes to the overall effectiveness of your letter. Ensure your cover letter is clear, concise, and professionally formatted to make the best possible impression on potential employers.

4. Making Your Cover Letter Stand Out

In a competitive job market, it's not enough for your cover letter to be well-structured; it must also stand out. This section will delve into strategies to make your cover letter memorable and compelling to potential employers, increasing your chances of securing an interview.

1) Tailoring to the Job

The first rule is to avoid generic letters. Tailor each cover letter to the specific job and company, showing that you have researched the company and understand its goals, culture, and challenges.

Also, highlight how your skills and experience directly address the job requirements and company needs.

2) Showcasing Your Unique Value

Identify and articulate what makes you different from other candidates. This could be a unique combination of skills, experience, or a particular achievement relevant to the job.

Share brief anecdotes or case studies that showcase your achievements. Use quantifiable results to demonstrate your impact.

3) Engaging and Concise Writing

Active Voice: Use an active voice to create a more engaging and direct tone.

Conciseness: Be concise. Your cover letter should be no longer than one page. Focus on the most relevant and impressive details.

4) Incorporating Keywords

Industry Keywords: Use relevant keywords from the job description. This not only shows that you are a good fit but also helps in getting past automated applicant tracking systems.

Skills and Qualifications: Highlight the specific skills and qualifications mentioned in the job listing, aligning them with your experience.

5) Visually Appealing Format

Professional Layout: Use a clear, professional layout. Ensure that your font and formatting match those of your resumé.

Whitespace: Use whitespace effectively to make your letter easy to read.

6) Proofreading and Editing

Error-Free: Ensure your cover letter is free from grammatical errors and typos. This reflects attention to detail and professionalism.

Feedback: Have someone else review your cover letter. Fresh eyes can catch errors and offer valuable feedback.

7) Personal Touch

Show Enthusiasm: Express genuine enthusiasm for the role and the company.

Personal Connection: If you have a personal connection to the company or its mission, briefly mention it. This can create a memorable impression.

Making your cover letter stand out requires a combination of personalized content, engaging writing, strategic usage of keywords, and professional formatting. By applying these strategies, you can create a compelling cover letter that captures the attention of potential employers and effectively communicates your fit for the role.

Here is an example of a cover letter for a marketing specialist position that illustrates the strategies mentioned for making your cover letter stand out.

Jane Doe

123 Main Street

City, State, Zip

Phone: (123) 456-7890

E-mail: jane.doe@example.com

[Today's Date]

Hiring Manager

ABC Corporation

456 Business Rd.

Business City, State, Zip

Dear Hiring Manager,

I am writing to express my interest in the marketing specialist position at ABC Corporation, as advertised on your careers page. With a Bachelor's degree in Marketing and over three years of experience in dynamic marketing roles, I have developed a comprehensive skill set that perfectly aligns with the requirements of this role. My background in developing and executing successful marketing campaigns, combined with my passion for data-driven strategies, positions me to significantly contribute to your team.

[Tailoring to the Job]

At XYZ Company, I spearheaded a digital marketing campaign that increased online engagement by 40% within six months, a testament to my strategic approach and my ability to align initiatives with company objectives. I have followed ABC Corporation's growth and am particularly impressed by your commitment to innovation and community engagement, values that resonate with my professional philosophy.

[Showcasing Your Unique Value]

What sets me apart is my proficiency in leveraging analytics to inform marketing strategies and my experience in managing cross-platform campaigns, from social media to e-mail marketing. For instance, I led a project team to revamp our e-mail marketing strategy, which resulted in a 30% increase in conversion rates. This achievement highlights not only my expertise in digital marketing but also my capacity to drive profitability and brand awareness.

[Engaging and Concise Writing]

I am eager to bring my background in crafting targeted marketing strategies and my proactive approach to problem-solving to the Marketing Specialist role at ABC Corporation. I am particularly excited about the opportunity to contribute to innovative marketing solutions that enhance your company's market presence and foster long-term growth.

[Incorporating Keywords]

Through my experiences, I have become adept at content creation, SEO optimization, and analytics, skills that align with the job description. My hands-on experience with CRM software and my ability to analyze consumer behavior patterns will allow me to contribute to your sales and marketing objectives effectively.

[Visually Appealing Format]

I have attached my resumé, which further outlines my achievements. I am looking forward to the possibility of discussing my application in more detail and available for an interview at your earliest convenience.

[Proofreading and Editing]

Thank you for considering my application. I am keen on the opportunity to contribute to ABC Corporation's success and to further develop my skills in a challenging and creative environment.

[Personal Touch]

Your company's innovative approach to marketing and commitment to community engagement are particularly appealing to me, as I have always valued creativity and social responsibility in my professional endeavors.

Warm regards,

Jane Doe

This cover letter is tailored specifically to the job and company, showcases the candidate's unique value through specific achievements, is written concisely with an engaging and professional tone, incorporates the keywords from the job description, follows a visually appealing format, and includes a personal touch expressing genuine enthusiasm for the role and the company.

5. Customizing Cover Letters for Different Roles

Each job role requires a unique set of skills and qualities. Hence, customizing your cover letter for different roles is essential to demonstrate your suitability for each specific position. This section will provide guidance on how to effectively tailor your cover letter to various job roles.

1) Understanding the Job Description

First, carefully read the job description to understand what the employer is looking for. Identify the key skills, experience, and qualifications required for the role.

Second, align your skills and experience with those mentioned in the job description, focusing on the most relevant ones.

Class Activity 4: *Analyze the following three job ads and identify the key skills, experience, and qualifications required for each role.*

Job Ad 1: Junior Software Developer

Company: Tech Innovations Inc.

Location: San Francisco, CA

About the Role:

We are seeking a passionate junior software developer to join our dynamic team. The ideal candidate will be involved in all aspects of the software development lifecycle, from design to deployment. This role offers the opportunity to work on cutting-edge technology projects and to grow within the company.

Responsibilities:

- Collaborate with the development team to design, develop, and implement software solutions.
- Assist in the maintenance and upgrading of existing software applications.
- Participate in code reviews to maintain high-quality code standards.

Requirements:

- Bachelor's degree in Computer Science, Information Technology, or a related field.
- Proficiency in programming languages such as Java, C++, or Python.
- Familiarity with software development methodologies, especially Agile and Scrum.
- Excellent problem-solving skills and attention to detail.

Preferred Skills:

- Experience with database management and SQL.
- Knowledge of web development technologies like HTML, CSS, and JavaScript.

- A portfolio of software projects or contributions to open-source projects is a plus.

Job Ad 2: Digital Marketing Coordinator

Company: Bright Futures Marketing

Location: New York, NY

Overview:

Bright Futures Marketing is looking for a digital marketing coordinator to help execute our online marketing strategies. This role involves content creation, social media management, and analyzing digital marketing campaigns' performance. The ideal candidate is a creative thinker with a knack for identifying trends and engaging with online communities.

Duties:

- Develop and manage content for our social media platforms, including Facebook, Instagram, and Twitter.
- Monitor and report on the performance of marketing campaigns and social media activity.
- Collaborate with the marketing team to create promotional materials and marketing campaigns.

Qualifications:

- Bachelor's degree in Marketing, Communications, or a related field.
- Strong understanding of digital marketing principles and social media platforms.
- Excellent writing, editing, and communication skills.
- Ability to analyze data and provide insights on campaign performance.

Desirable Experience:

- Previous experience in a digital marketing role.
- Proficiency with digital marketing tools and software, such as Google Analytics and Hootsuite.
- Experience in SEO/SEM and e-mail marketing campaigns.

Job Ad 3: Environmental Scientist

Organization: Green Earth Conservation

Location: Denver, CO

Position Summary:

Green Earth Conservation seeks a dedicated environmental scientist to join our team. The successful candidate will conduct field research, analyze environmental data, and contribute to conservation projects. This role is ideal for someone passionate about environmental protection and sustainability.

Key Responsibilities:

- Conduct field research and collect data on environmental conditions.
- Analyze data to identify trends, issues, and solutions for environmental conservation.
- Prepare reports and present findings to stakeholders and the public.

Requirements:

- Bachelor's or Master's degree in Environmental Science, Ecology, or a related field.
- Strong analytical skills and proficiency in statistical analysis software.
- Knowledge of environmental laws and regulations.

Preferred Qualifications:

- Experience in conducting field research and data analysis.
- Familiarity with geographic information system technology.
- Excellent written and verbal communication skills.

2) Industry-Specific Language

First, demonstrating familiarity with industry-specific terminology can show that you are knowledgeable and well-suited for the role.

Second, the tone of your cover letter should match the industry's culture. For instance, a creative industry might appreciate a more informal and creative tone, while a legal position may require a more formal style.

Here is an example of a cover letter using the industry-specific language to apply for the job in Job Ad 2, Class Activity 4.

> **[Your Name]**
> [Your Address]
> [City, State, Zip]
> [Your Phone Number]
> [Your E-mail Address]
> [Today's Date]

Hiring Manager
Bright Futures Marketing
[Company Address]
New York, NY

Dear Hiring Manager,

I am writing to express my enthusiasm for the digital marketing coordinator position at Bright Futures Marketing, as advertised on your company website. With a Bachelor's degree in Marketing from [University Name] and over two years of hands-on experience in digital marketing roles, I have honed my skills in content creation, social media management, and campaign analysis, making me an ideal fit for your dynamic team.

At my current position with [Current Company Name], I have successfully developed and implemented digital marketing strategies that increased our social media engagement by 50% and website traffic by 30% within six months. My approach always starts with a deep understanding of brand objectives, followed by creative content creation tailored to engage specific target audiences across platforms like Facebook, Instagram, and Twitter.

I am particularly drawn to Bright Futures Marketing due to your innovative approach to online engagement and your commitment to utilizing digital platforms to achieve marketing goals. I am eager to bring my expertise in leveraging tools such as Google Analytics and Hootsuite to monitor campaign performance and adapt strategies to maximize results. My proficiency in SEO/SEM, along with my ability to analyze data to inform content strategies, aligns with the qualifications you are seeking for this role.

In addition to my professional experience, I have strong writing, editing, and communication skills, essential for developing compelling marketing materials and fostering effective team collaboration. I am particularly proud of a recent project where I led a cross-functional team to launch a targeted e-mail marketing campaign, resulting in a 40% increase in engagement and a 25% increase in sales over three months.

I am enthusiastic about the opportunity to contribute to Bright Futures Marketing's success by driving more meaningful engagements through innovative digital marketing strategies. I look forward to the possibility of discussing this exciting opportunity with you. Thank you for considering my application. I am hopeful for an interview to further discuss how I can contribute to your team.

Warm regards,

[Your Name]

This cover letter incorporates the industry-specific language and concepts, demonstrating the candidate's familiarity with digital marketing tools and strategies. It also aligns the candidate's skills and experience with the job description, emphasizing his or her ability to contribute to the company's marketing goals.

3) Highlighting Relevant Experience

Choose examples from your work history that are most relevant to the job role. Highlight projects, achievements, or roles that closely relate to the potential job's requirements. Where possible, use numbers and statistics to quantify your successes in previous roles, as this can be particularly persuasive.

Here is an example of a cover letter demonstrating how to tailor relevant experience to meet the specific demands of a software development role.

[Your Name]

[Your Address]

[City, State, Zip]

[Your Phone Number]

[Your E-mail Address]

[Today's Date]

Hiring Manager

Tech Innovations Inc.

[Company Address]

San Francisco, CA

Dear Hiring Manager,

I am excited to submit my application for the junior software developer position at Tech Innovations Inc., as advertised on your company's career page. With a Bachelor's degree in Computer Science from [University Name] and hands-on experience in software development projects, I am eager to bring my skills in Java, C++, and Python programming to your innovative team.

During my internship at [Previous Company Name], I had the opportunity to contribute to a major project focused on developing a new inventory management software. My role involved collaborating closely with the development team to design and implement robust software solutions that improved inventory accuracy by 20%. This experience not only sharpened my programming skills but also taught me the value of clear communication and teamwork in achieving project goals.

I am particularly drawn to the position at Tech Innovations Inc. because of your commitment to using cutting-edge technology to solve real-world problems. I am impressed by your recent project [mention any known project of the company], and I am enthusiastic about the opportunity to contribute to such impactful work.

At [University Name], I completed a capstone project where I led a team in developing a web application that streamlined event planning for college organizations. This project, which was developed using Agile methodologies, allowed me to deepen my understanding of the software development lifecycle and further develop my skills in web development technologies like HTML, CSS, and JavaScript. It was during this time that I learned the importance of iterative development and user feedback in creating effective software solutions.

I am confident that my academic background, combined with my practical experience, makes me a strong candidate for the junior software developer role. I am particularly excited about the possibility of working in an environment that values innovative solutions and encourages continuous learning and professional growth.

Thank you for considering my application. I look forward to the opportunity to discuss how my education, skills, and experience align with the needs of Tech Innovations Inc. I am available at your convenience for an interview and can be reached at [Your Phone Number] or via e-mail at [Your E-mail Address].

Warmest regards,

[Your Name]

This cover letter is tailored to highlight the candidate's relevant experience in software development, emphasizing his or her proficiency in the required programming languages and methodologies, as mentioned in the job ad. It also demonstrates the candidate's enthusiasm for the role and the company, making a compelling case for his or her candidacy.

4) Addressing the Company's Needs

Understand the company's mission, values, and current challenges. Tailor your cover letter to address how you can contribute to these areas.

Express your enthusiasm for the role and the company. Make it clear why you are particularly interested in working for them.

5) Role-Specific Qualities

If applying for a leadership position, emphasize your experience that demonstrates leadership, strategic planning, and team management.

For technical positions, focus on specific technologies, methodologies, or projects you have worked on, detailing your expertise.

In creative fields, discuss your creative process, showcase innovative ideas, and potentially include links to a portfolio.

6) Closing with a Call to Action

Conclude by expressing your readiness to further discuss how your skills and experience align with the role during an interview.

Mention that you will follow up if appropriate, showing your proactive nature and keen interest in the position.

Here is an example of a cover letter demonstrating the candidate's understanding of the job's requirements and his or her eagerness to contribute to the organization's goals.

[Your Name]
[Your Address]
[City, State, Zip]
[Your Phone Number]
[Your E-mail Address]
[Today's Date]
Hiring Manager
Green Earth Conservation
[Company Address]
Denver, CO

Dear Hiring Manager,

I am writing to express my interest in the environmental scientist position at Green Earth Conservation, as advertised. With a Master's degree in Environmental Science from [University Name] and over four years of experience in field research and data analysis related to conservation efforts, I am excited about the opportunity to

---

contribute to your team's mission to protect and sustain the natural environment.

In my current role at [Current Company Name], I led a project focused on assessing the impacts of urban development on local wildlife habitats. My team and I conducted comprehensive field research, which included collecting and analyzing soil, water, and biodiversity samples over a two-year period. Our findings contributed to the development of community guidelines that successfully balanced development needs with environmental conservation, showcasing my commitment to creating solutions that serve both the ecosystem and local communities.

I understand that Green Earth Conservation is at the forefront of addressing critical environmental issues through innovative research and sustainable practices. I am particularly impressed by your recent initiative [mention any specific project or initiative of the company], which aligns with my professional expertise and personal values. I am eager to bring my skills in statistical analysis and GIS technology to support your ongoing and future projects, particularly in areas requiring in-depth environmental impact assessments and sustainable resource management strategies.

My experience has equipped me with a robust skill set in environmental data analysis, project management, and stakeholder communication. I have consistently demonstrated the ability to interpret complex data and translate it into actionable insights and strategies. I am confident that my background can contribute significantly to the impactful work being done at Green Earth Conservation.

I am enthusiastic about the possibility of joining your team and contributing to your mission of fostering a sustainable future. I look forward to the opportunity to discuss how my education, experience, and skills can support Green Earth Conservation's objectives. Please feel free to contact me at [Your Phone Number] or via e-mail at [Your E-mail Address] to arrange an interview.

Thank you for considering my application. I am keen on the opportunity to make a meaningful contribution to your esteemed organization and to further discuss how I can assist in advancing your conservation efforts.

Sincerely,

[Your Name]

Customizing your cover letter for different roles is crucial in your job search. It demonstrates to the employer that you have taken the time to understand both the role and their company, and have thoughtfully considered how you can contribute. By tailoring your approach, you increase your chances of standing out as an ideal candidate for each unique position.

Class Activity 5: *Write a cover letter according to the following steps.*

Step 1: Researching and Tailoring

Choose a real or fictional job listing. Research the company's culture, values, and recent projects. Write a paragraph that demonstrates your understanding of the company and how your skills and experience align with their needs.

Step 2: Highlighting Your Unique Value Proposition

Write a brief section of a cover letter that highlights an achievement or skill that makes you particularly well-suited for the job you're applying for. Use quantifiable results to back up your claims.

Step 3: Addressing the Company's Needs

Given a job ad (real or fictional), identify the company's three main needs or problems they wish to solve with this hire. Write three sentences for a cover letter, each addressing one of these needs with a solution or example from your past experience.

Step 4: Engaging and Concise Writing

Write a long, detailed paragraph for a cover letter and rewrite it to be more concise, aiming to reduce its length by at least 50% without losing the essential information.

Step 5: Incorporating Keywords

Identify the keywords from a job ad and use them to write a cover letter paragraph. Ensure the paragraph sounds natural and not forced.

Step 6: Visually Appealing Format

Use a word processing program to format a cover letter. Focus on font choice, margins, spacing, and the use of bullet points for a list of achievements. Share with a peer for feedback.

Step 7: Proofreading and Editing

Exchange your cover letter with a peer. Each person will proofread the other's cover letter, marking errors and suggesting improvements. Discuss the feedback together.

Step 8: Closing with a Call to Action

Write a closing paragraph for a cover letter that includes a polite call to action, encouraging the hiring manager to contact you for an interview. Ensure it conveys enthusiasm and confidence.

Step 9: Group Discussion

After completing these steps, have a group discussion about the challenges of writing cover letters and share insights gained from the exercises. Discuss which strategies were most helpful and how these exercises have changed the way you write the cover letter.

7.2
Writing for Social Media

In the digital age, social media has become a powerful tool for businesses to connect with their audience, build brand awareness, and engage in meaningful conversations. Writing for social media requires a distinct approach, combining conciseness, creativity, and the ability to spark immediate interest. This section will delve into useful strategies for crafting effective social media content that captivates your audience and aligns with your brand's voice.

7.2.1 Understanding Social Media Platforms

This section will explore the landscape of social media, focusing on the most popular platforms. Each platform has its unique audience, content format, and communication style. Understanding these differences is key to effectively engaging with your audience and crafting messages that resonate.

Major social media platforms are introduced as follows:

- **Facebook:** The largest social networking site, where users can post text, photos, and videos, create events, and engage in groups. Facebook's audience is broad, making it a versatile platform for many types of content.

- **X (former Twitter):** Known for its brevity, Twitter allows for quick, concise messages called tweets. It's a prime platform for real-time updates, trending topics, and hashtags to join broader conversations.

- **Instagram:** A visually-driven platform focused on photos and videos, ideal for brands and individuals who want to tell their story through imagery. Instagram Stories and Reels offer more dynamic ways to engage with followers.

- **LinkedIn:** The professional networking site where content is more formal and business-oriented. It's the go-to platform for industry news, professional development, and networking.

- **TikTok:** A rapidly growing platform for short-form, creative video content. Its algorithm favors high-engagement content, making it a powerful tool for reaching a younger audience.

Mastering the writing skills for social media involves understanding the nuances of each platform. By tailoring your message to fit the specific audience, format, and community engagement style of each platform, you can create more effective and impactful content.

Class Activity 6: *List one or two social media platforms and discuss their features with your classmates.*

7.2.2 Developing a Voice and Tone

Developing a consistent voice and tone for your social media presence is crucial for building brand identity and establishing trust with your audience. This section will explore how to define your voice and adapt your tone to fit different situations and platforms.

1. Understanding Voice and Tone

Your voice is the personality of your brand or personal social media presence. It's consistent across all messages and content you create. Your voice could be professional, friendly, whimsical, authoritative, or any combination that aligns with your brand identity.

Tone, on the other hand, is the mood or attitude of an individual message. It can vary depending on the context, platform, or audience's mood. For example, your tone might be more serious when discussing industry news on LinkedIn and more playful or casual on Instagram.

2. Establishing Your Voice

Identify Your Core Values: Begin by identifying the core values and personality traits you want your brand to embody. Are you innovative, compassionate, authoritative, educational, or entertaining?

Analyze Your Audience: Understand who your audience are, including their demographics, interests, and what they seek from your content. Tailoring your voice to resonate with your audience increases engagement.

Study Competitors: Look at how competitors or similar profiles communicate. Note what works and what doesn't, but ensure your voice remains unique.

Create a Voice Chart: Develop a voice chart that outlines your brand's personality traits, do's and don'ts, and examples of how your voice should be applied in different types of content.

3. Adapting Your Tone

Platform Considerations: Adjust your tone to suit the platform you're using. For example, messages on LinkedIn often have a more professional tone, while tweets can afford to be lighter and more humorous.

Audience Mood: Be mindful of the current mood or concerns of your audience. For instance, during challenging times, a more empathetic and supportive tone is appropriate.

Content Context: The tone should also match the context of your content. Promotional content might have an excited tone, while educational content might adopt a more informative and straightforward tone.

4. Voice and Tone Guidelines

Consistency Is Key: While your tone might shift slightly depending on the context, your underlying voice should remain consistent to build brand identity and trust.

Be Authentic: Authenticity resonates with the audience. Ensure your voice aligns with your brand's values and mission.

Flexibility Within Framework: Have a clear framework for your voice and tone but allow flexibility for real-time engagement and trends.

Feedback and Evolution: Regularly solicit feedback from your audience to refine your voice and tone. Social media trends and audience expectations evolve, and so should your approach.

Class Activity 7: *There are three pieces of writing for different brands and the voice characteristics of Brand 1 have been identified. Identify the voice characteristics of the rest two brands.*

Brand 1: Outdoor Adventure Gear Company

Post: Embrace the wild with every step. Our latest eco-friendly hiking boots are here to journey with you, from the untamed paths to the peaks that touch the sky.

AdventureBeginsHere

Voice Characteristics:

- Adventurous: Use words like "embrace the wild" and "untamed paths" to evoke a sense of adventure.

- Eco-conscious: Highlight the eco-friendly aspect of their products, appealing to environmentally-aware consumers.

- Inspirational: Aim to inspire with imagery of journeys and reaching peaks.

Brand 2: Luxury Fashion Brand

Post: Elegance redefined. Our Autumn Collection merges timeless sophistication with modern silhouettes, crafted for the discerning. Discover the essence of luxury. #TimelessElegance

Voice Characteristics: _____

_____

Brand 3: Health and Wellness Start-Up

Post: Start your morning with a burst of energy! Our SuperGreen Smoothie packs are filled with all the nutrients you need to kickstart your day. Healthy living made easy and delicious! #GreenEnergy

Voice Characteristics: _____

_____

Class Activity 8: *Find some social media posts from different brands and write down the voice characteristics that stand out to you. Explain the reasons why these characteristics align with the brand's identity and audience expectations.*

Class Activity 9: *The following are a list of brand descriptions on the left and a set of social media posts on the right. Match each post to the brand based on the voice used. Then give your reasons.*

Brand A: A luxury watchmaker known for its timeless design and precision craftsmanship. The brand prides itself on tradition and has been a symbol of elegance and status for over a century.

Post 1: Elevate your daily routine with the power of nature. Our all-natural, plant-based cleaners are here to make your home sparkle without the plastic waste. #EcoClean #GreenLiving"

Brand B: A vibrant start-up focused on eco-friendly cleaning products. They are passionate about reducing plastic waste and use only natural, plant-based ingredients in their products.

Post 2: Discover the art of precision. Our latest collection marries traditional craftsmanship with unparalleled elegance. Experience luxury that stands the test of time. #TimelessElegance #LuxuryWatches

Brand C: A cutting-edge fitness app that uses AI to create personalized workout plans. It targets tech-savvy individuals looking to optimize their fitness routine with the latest technology.

Post 3: Transform your workout with AI. Our app tailors every exercise to your personal fitness goals, making every session smarter, not harder. #TechFitness #PersonalizedTraining

Class Activity 10: *Choose an industry or a hypothetical brand and develop a set of voice characteristics that would suit it. Then write a social media post that exemplifies this voice.*

Class Activity 11: *Take a generic social media post and rewrite it in three different voices, each representing a different brand personality (e.g., professional, playful, and compassionate). Notice how the changing of the voice affects the impact and audience perception of the message.*

5. Consistent Voice

Your voice is the constant persona behind your social media presence, while your tone can vary depending on the context, platform, and audience. Developing a clear voice and adaptable tone strategy is essential for engaging effectively with your audience across various social media platforms. By staying authentic, consistent, and responsive to feedback, you can establish a strong, recognizable brand presence that resonates with your audience.

The following is an example of using language and tone to establish a brand voice.

Brand: UrbanStyle—a trendy fashion retailer

Inconsistent Brand Voice	**Consistent Brand Voice**
Social media post 1 (Facebook):	Social media post 1 (Facebook):
Hey everyone! Check out our new collection. It's totally awesome!	Hello, fashion enthusiasts! Feast your eyes on our latest collection, meticulously designed to capture urban vibes and your unique style. Explore now!
Social media post 2 (Twitter):	Social media post 2 (Twitter):
New collection just dropped! So lit! #Fashion #Trendy	Unveiling our freshest collection, curated to celebrate urban fashion in all its glory. Embrace the trendsetter in you! #UrbanStyle
Social media post 3 (Instagram):	Social media post 3 (Instagram):
Introducing our latest collection, inspired by urban vibes. Get ready to slay the streets! #UrbanStyle	Step into the world of urban chic with our newest collection. Each piece tells a story of modern aesthetics and self-expression. Elevate your style game! #UrbanStyle

The posts from the left column are inconsistent with the brand voice, while those from the right column are consistent with the brand UrbanStyle for the following reasons:

- **Tone and Language:** In the left column, the tone and language vary significantly across the posts. The first post is casual ("Hey everyone!"), the second is informal and uses slang ("So lit!"), and the third is a mix of casual and slightly more formal. This inconsistency can confuse the audience about the brand's identity. In the right column, each post maintains a sophisticated and fashion-forward tone. The language is consistently elegant and polished, reflecting a high-end, trendy fashion retailer's style.

- **Target Audience Engagement:** In the left column, the style of communication seems to target different audience segments in each post, from very casual and youthful to slightly more mature. In the right column, all posts seem to target the same audience—fashion enthusiasts who appreciate urban, chic, and sophisticated fashion. The language used is more likely to resonate with an audience interested in high-fashion and urban trends.

- **Brand Identity Representation:** In the left column, there's a lack of a clear, unified theme or message that ties the posts together. The varying styles do not consistently communicate a coherent brand identity. In the right column, each post reinforces the brand's identity as a trendy, urban fashion retailer. The consistent focus on "urban chic" and "modern aesthetics" helps strengthen the brand's identity.

- **Messaging and Visual Imagery:** In the left column, the messaging is varied and doesn't follow a uniform pattern. The first post is overly casual, the second is trendy but lacks depth, and the third is descriptive but lacks the sophistication of the brand. In the right column, the messaging consistently emphasizes urban fashion, chic style, and personal expression, which aligns with the brand's image. The language evokes a visual imagery consistent with the brand's aesthetic.

In summary, the right column's posts are consistent as they maintain a uniform tone, engage the target audience effectively, represent the brand identity clearly, and provide cohesive messaging and visual imagery, all of which are crucial for a consistent brand voice, especially for a trendy fashion retailer like UrbanStyle. By maintaining a consistent brand voice, UrbanStyle effectively communicates its unique identity, values, and offerings across various social media platforms. This ensures that every interaction with their audience is on-brand, enhancing engagement, loyalty, and overall impact.

7.2.3 Creating Engaging Content

Creating engaging content is vital for capturing the attention of your audience on social media and encouraging interaction. This section will provide useful strategies for crafting compelling posts that resonate with followers and foster a sense of community.

1. Crafting Captivating Posts

Headlines and Hooks: Begin with a strong headline or opening sentence that can grab the attention of readers. Pose a question, state an intriguing fact, or lead with a bold statement to hook readers immediately.

Storytelling: Use storytelling to connect with readers on an emotional level. Share customer testimonials, behind-the-scenes stories, or brand journey narratives that make your content relatable and memorable.

Visual Appeal: Enhance posts with high-quality images, videos, or infographics that complement your text and are visually appealing. Visuals are often the first element that readers notice. Create the content that encourages likes, shares, and interactions.

To illustrate how these strategies come together in a real-world example, let's take a look at a social media post designed to engage the audience and boost interaction.

Example: Social Media Post (Instagram)

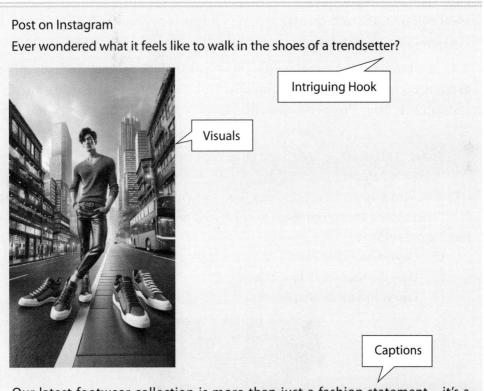

Post on Instagram
Ever wondered what it feels like to walk in the shoes of a trendsetter?

Intriguing Hook

Visuals

Captions

Our latest footwear collection is more than just a fashion statement—it's a journey into the heart of urban chic. From sleek sneakers to bold boots, each pair is a masterpiece of style and comfort. Ready to make the streets your runway? Explore the collection now! #StepIntoStyle #UrbanTrendsetters #FashionForward #UrbanStyle

Hashtags

This post is designed to engage the audience, encourage interactions (likes, shares, or comments), and increase brand visibility and identity reinforcement on social media platforms.

2. Driving Engagement

Calls to Action (CTAs): Include clear CTAs that encourage your audience to take the next step, whether it's commenting, sharing, visiting a website, or making a purchase.

Interactive Content: Create polls, quizzes, and contests that invite participation. Interactive content not only engages but can also provide valuable insights into your audience's preferences.

Relevance and Timeliness: Publish the content that's relevant to current events, trends, or seasonal topics. Timeliness can increase the likelihood of your content being shared and becoming part of larger conversations.

Example: Engaging Social Media Post

To see how these strategies can come to life, let's look at an example from "FitFusion", a health and fitness company. This Instagram post demonstrates how a brand can effectively drive engagement.

Brand: "FitFusion"—a health and fitness company

Post on Instagram

Ready to transform your fitness journey? Embrace the #FitFusionChallenge!
□♀□Join us for a 30-day challenge to crush your goals and elevate your energy levels. Here's what's in store:

- ☐ Customized Meal Plans
- ☐ Daily Workouts with Pro Trainers
- ☐ Expert Tips for Lasting Results

> Tag your workout buddy and conquer this challenge together! Let's break a sweat, have fun, and make lasting changes. □#FitFusion #FitnessJourney #GetFitTogether

The post is engaging in the following ways:

- **Clear Call to Action:** The post invites followers to join the challenge, making it easy for them to participate.

- **Benefits Highlight:** It outlines the benefits of the challenge, addressing the audience's potential concerns.

- **Visual Appeal:** The use of emojis and visually appealing formatting captures attention while emphasizing key points.

- **Inclusivity:** The call to tag a workout buddy encourages community engagement and participation.

- **Urgency and Excitement:** The use of phrases like "Ready to transform..." and "Let's break a sweat" adds energy and urgency.

- **Hashtags:** Relevant hashtags increase discoverability and help the post reach a wider audience.

By crafting the engaging content, FitFusion effectively encourages its audience to not only like and share the post but also actively participate in the fitness challenge. This not only increases engagement metrics but also creates a sense of community and loyalty among its followers.

7.2.4 Tailoring Content to Platforms

Adapt your content to suit the unique features of each platform.

1. Facebook

Audience: Diverse, with a significant number of users across various age groups.

Content Features: Support a wide range of content, including text, photos, videos, etc. Facebook is great for detailed posts, community building, and event promotion.

Strategy: Use a more conversational tone, engage with followers through comments, and create community-focused content like groups and events.

2. X (former Twitter)

Audience: Broad, with a focus on real-time information and trending topics.

Content Features: Character limit per tweet, emphasizing concise and catchy messages. Ideal for news, quick updates, and direct interactions with followers.

Strategy: Post frequent updates, engage in trending topics, use hashtags effectively, and maintain a dynamic and timely presence.

3. Instagram

Audience: Skew younger, visually oriented users.

Content Features: Highly visual platform focusing on images and videos, with features like Stories, Reels, and IGTV.

Strategy: Use high-quality visuals, maintain a consistent aesthetic, use Stories for behind-the-scenes content, and leverage influencers for broader reach.

4. LinkedIn

Audience: Professionals and business-oriented users.

Content Features: Focus on professional content, networking, and career development. Support articles, standard posts, and professional updates.

Strategy: Share industry insights, company news, professional achievements, and thought leadership content. Networking and building professional relationships are key.

5. Xiaohongshu (RED)

Audience: Primarily young, urban Chinese users, heavily skewed towards lifestyle, beauty, and fashion content.

Content Features: Known for its blend of lifestyle blogging and e-commerce. Users share product reviews, shopping experiences, and lifestyle stories.

Strategy: Focus on high-quality visuals and storytelling. Content should be authentic and relatable, and provide value, such as tutorials, reviews, or lifestyle tips. Influencer collaborations can be particularly effective.

In summary, each platform requires a distinct approach to content creation and engagement. Understanding the unique features and audiences of each platform is crucial for crafting effective social media strategies. For example:

- **Twitter:** Embrace brevity and make every character count.
- **Instagram:** Focus on visuals, using captivating images and concise captions.

- **LinkedIn:** Maintain a professional tone while sharing industry insights.

The following social media posts demonstrate the strategy of adapting the content to suit the unique features of each platform.

Brand: TechTrend—sharing technology news and insights

> **In Twitter:**
> Exciting news in tech! Unveiling the latest breakthrough in AI. Learn how it's reshaping industries and sparking innovation. #TechTrend #AIRevolution

The post uses the concise language to convey excitement and introduces the topic efficiently within Twitter's character limit.

> **In LinkedIn:**
> Exploring the AI revolution: Join us in delving into how artificial intelligence is disrupting industries, boosting efficiency, and paving the way for new possibilities. Let's shape the future of tech together. #TechTrend #AIInsights

The post adopts a professional tone and explicitly invites industry insights and collaboration, aligning with LinkedIn's audience of professionals.

By tailoring content to each platform, "TechTrend" maximizes engagement and resonates with the specific preferences and expectations of users on Twitter, Instagram, and LinkedIn. This approach ensures the brand's message is effectively conveyed on each platform, optimizing the impact of its communication efforts.

7.2.5 Utilizing User-Generated Content

Encourage users to create content about your brand, including:

- **Contests and Challenges:** Invite users to participate in creative challenges.
- **Testimonials:** Share positive feedback from customers.

The following is an example of utilizing user-generated content.

Brand: TastyBites—sharing food and recipe blogs

Contests and Challenges:

☐ Calling all foodies! It's time for the #TastyBites RecipeChallenge! Create a mouthwatering dish using your favorite ingredients and share the recipe with us. Tag us and use the hashtag for a chance to be featured on our page and win exciting prizes. Let your culinary creativity shine!

> The brand encourages its audience to participate in a creative challenge that aligns with their interests. The contest fosters engagement and generates user-generated content related to the brand's niche.

Testimonials:

☐ TastyBites has transformed my cooking game! Their recipes are not only delicious but also easy to follow. I've become the go-to chef among my friends thanks to their tips. Highly recommend!—Jane D., Food Enthusiast

> Sharing a genuine customer testimonial adds authenticity and builds trust among the audience. It showcases the positive impact of the brand on real individuals.

By utilizing the user-generated content strategy, TastyBites engages its audience in meaningful ways. The recipe challenge sparks creativity and participation, while the testimonials showcase the brand's positive influence, encouraging others to engage with the brand's content and offerings.

7.2.6 Responding to Comments and Messages

Engage with your audience by promptly responding to comments and messages, including:

- **Acknowledgment:** Show appreciation for positive comments.
- **Problem-Solving:** Address customers' concerns and queries.

The following is an example of responding to comments and messages.

Brand: Wanderlust Adventures—a travel agency

Acknowledgment:

Comment from User: "Just booked my dream vacation with #WanderlustAdventures! Can't wait to explore!"

Brand's Response: "We're thrilled to be part of your dream adventure! Get ready for unforgettable experiences and breathtaking moments. Safe travels! "

> The brand acknowledges the user's excitement and expresses gratitude, fostering a positive interaction and building a connection.

The following is an example of problem-solving.

Comment from User: "Experiencing issues with my booking. Haven't received confirmation."

Brand's Response: We apologize for the inconvenience, [User]. Please check your inbox for a direct message from us. We'll ensure your booking is sorted out promptly.

> The brand promptly addresses the user's concern, offers a solution, and assures him or her of assistance through direct messaging, showcasing proactive customer service.

By responding to comments and messages, Wanderlust Adventures strengthens its customer relationships. The brand's appreciation for positive feedback enhances positive sentiment, while addressing issues promptly demonstrates a commitment to customer satisfaction and problem-solving.

Writing for social media demands a dynamic blend of creativity, strategy, and responsiveness. By applying these strategies, you'll create content that not only resonates with your audience but also strengthens your brand's online presence.

7.3
Writing for Public Relations

In the realm of business, maintaining a positive public image and effective communication with various stakeholders are essential. Building public relations involves crafting messages that shape perceptions, manage crises, and build strong relationships. This section will explore useful strategies and techniques for writing impactful public relations content that fosters goodwill, establishes credibility, and enhances brand reputation.

7.3.1 The Role of Public Relations

The role of public relations is multifaceted and central to the way an organization presents itself to the world. At its core, public relations is about image building; it involves crafting and disseminating narratives that portray the organization in a positive light, thereby shaping public perception. Another critical aspect is crisis management, which entails addressing and mitigating negative situations as swiftly and efficiently as possible to minimize any potential damage to the organization's reputation. Moreover, public relations is responsible for stakeholder communication, which includes engaging with a diverse group of stakeholders such as clients, employees, media, and investors. This engagement is crucial for maintaining strong relationships and ensuring that all parties are informed and aligned with the organization's goals and values.

To summarize, public relations involves:

- **Image Building:** Crafting narratives that portray the organization in a positive light.

- **Crisis Management:** Addressing and mitigating negative situations swiftly.

- **Stakeholder Communication:** Engaging with clients, employees, media, and investors.

Here is an example of an effective press release for crisis management. When Volkswagen designed computer software to hide the true amount of emissions from their vehicles, they needed to find a way to calm their shareholders, acknowledge their error, and reassure the public of their resolve in the face of a crisis.

US Media Site
MATTHIAS MÜLLER:"WE WILL OVERCOME THIS CRISIS"
Oct. 6, 2015
- Group CEO addresses Wolfsburg employees at works meeting
- Müller announces swift and relentless clarification of emissions scandal
- Müller:"We will do everything we can to ensure that Volkswagen continues to stand for good and secure jobs in the future"
- EU6 diesel vehicles comply with legal specifications and environmental requirements
- Technical solutions for customers are imminent
- Care is even more important than speed—Müller:"We are dealing with four brands and many model variants"

- Efficiency program to be intensified—further critical review of all planned investments

Speaking at a works meeting in Wolfsburg today the CEO of Volkswagen Aktiengesellschaft, Matthias Müller, promised employees "swift and relentless clarification" of the emissions scandal. He said that what had happened went against everything the Group and its people stand for and that there was no excuse. At the same time, he encouraged employees to take heart: "We can and we will overcome this crisis, because Volkswagen is a group with a strong foundation. And above all because we have the best automobile team anyone could wish for." He added that the company would do everything it could to ensure that Volkswagen continues to stand for good and secure jobs in the future.

Speaking to more than 20,000 employees in Hall 11 at the Wolfsburg plant, Müller made it clear that "apart from the enormous financial damage which it is still not possible to quantify as of today, this crisis is first and foremost a crisis of confidence. That is because it is about the very core of our company and our identity: It is about our vehicles." Müller went on to say that solidity, reliability and credibility belong to the essence of the Volkswagen brand: "Our most important task will therefore be to win back the trust we have lost—with our customers, partners, investors and the general public." According to Müller, the first step toward achieving that was swift and relentless clarification. "Only when everything has been put on the table, when no single stone has been left unturned, only then will people begin to trust us again," Müller said.

The CEO asked employees for their understanding, saying that he, too, did not yet have the answer to many questions: "Believe me—like you, I am impatient. But in this situation, where we are dealing with four brands and many model variants care is even more important than speed."

This press release did just that. They acknowledged the violation of people's trust, doing so honestly and humbly, which recognized the significance of their actions.

The following is another great example of a crisis management press release. Data breaches happen quite frequently in the business world, and can have serious consequences. In this press release, the shop chain Target reassured people that they were fully investigating what happened to stop it from happening again. It also confirms that payment information was not at risk. There is also a call to action on what to do if you have been impacted, with clear contact details provided. A press release of this nature can also take the time to remind customers of the history they share with the firm.

> Target Provides Update on Data Breach and Financial Performance
> MNNEAPOLIS—January 10,2014
>
> Target today announced updates on its continuing investigation into the recent data breach and its expected fourth quarter financial performance.
>
> As part of Target's ongoing forensic investigation, it has been determined that certain guest information—separate from the payment card data previously disclosed—was taken during the data breach.
>
> This theft is not a new breach, but was uncovered as part of the ongoing investigation. At this time, the investigation has determined that the stolen information includes names, mailing addresses, phone numbers or e-mail addresses for up to 70 million individuals.
>
> Much of this data is partial in nature, but in cases where Target has an email address, the Company will attempt to contact affected guests. This communication will be informational, including tips to guard against consumer scams. Target will not ask those guests to provide any personal information as part of that communication. In addition, guests can find the tips on our website.
>
> "I know that it is frustrating for our guests to learn that this information was taken and we are truly sorry they are having to endure this,"said Gregg Steirhafel chairman.

7.3.2 Tailoring Messages

In the realm of public relations, the adaptation of messages to suit different audiences is crucial. For the media, this involves drafting press releases and statements that not only provide accurate information but also contain newsworthy elements to capture journalists' attention. When communicating with customers, the messaging shifts to focus on product updates, notable achievements, and upcoming events that might be of interest to the consumer base. Meanwhile, for investors, the communication must center around financial reports, strategic direction, and growth plans, providing a transparent view of the organization's financial health and future prospects. Each audience demands a tailored approach to ensure the message is both received and perceived in the intended manner.

To summarize, public relations messages should be adapted to the following different audiences:

- **Media:** Drafting press releases and statements that provide accurate and newsworthy information.
- **Customers:** Communicating product updates, achievements, and events.
- **Investors:** Sharing financial reports, strategies, and growth plans.

7.3.3　Crafting Press Releases

When crafting a press release, it's essential to start with a strong headline that captures the essence of the news in an engaging manner, drawing in readers right from the outset. The body of the release should promptly answer the fundamental questions of who, what, when, where, and why, ideally within the first few paragraphs to quickly inform the readers of the critical details. Additionally, incorporating quotes from company officials or relevant experts is important as it adds a layer of credibility to the release, providing a human element and authoritative perspectives on the matter at hand.

To summarize, a press release should:

- Begin with a strong headline—Summarize the news in a captivating way.
- Answer the 5W's—address who, what, when, where, and why in the opening paragraphs.
- Include quotes—include statements from company officials or experts to add credibility.

The following is an example of product launch or improvement press release. This press release tells the audience about a new (or improved) product being launched. The idea is to focus on what makes this product different from your competitors and sell its benefits.

Smart Robotics Expands Smart Palletizer Cobot Line to Optimize Box Stacking

Smart Robotics has launched three newly engineered versions of its collaborative robot system to increase item stacking efficiency.

By Robotics 24/7 Staff　· ⏱ September 8, 2022　· ⏏ in 🐦 f

Smart Robotics today announced three new versions of its Smart Palletizer collaborative robot system. The Eindhoven, Netherlands-based company said its newly engineered offerings will offer warehouses more options to automate and optimize warehouses in response to growing labor shortages.

"Since the Smart Palletizer can take over physically demanding, repetitive tasks, we're pleased to introduce our new product line to the market to be able to serve a larger audience," stated Johan Jardevall, CEO of Smart Robotics. He added that it's part of "our mission to lessen the pressure on warehouse employees' risk to their overall health".

The headline tells the audience what the new product is and its main benefit. There is a direct quote from the CEO, and further benefits are provided highlighting the superiority of the latest products, including directly informing the staff how it will make life easier and less risky for them than previously. The visual provided shows the product in action.

The following is another example of press release.

Company: InnoTech Solutions—an innovative tech start-up

InnoTech Solutions Unveils Revolutionary AI-Powered Software for Streamlining Business Operations

City, Date—InnoTech Solutions, a trailblazing tech start-up, is proud to announce the launch of their cutting-edge AI-powered software, OptiStream. This innovative solution aims to transform how businesses manage and optimize their operations, ushering in a new era of efficiency and productivity.

Streamlining Operations with AI Precision

OptiStream leverages advanced artificial intelligence algorithms to analyze complex operational data and provide real-time insights. From inventory management to supply chain optimization, the software empowers organizations to make data-driven decisions, reduce wastage, and enhance overall performance.

Empowering Businesses for Success

"Our team is excited to introduce OptiStream, a culmination of relentless innovation and technological prowess," said Jane Smith, co-founder and CEO of InnoTech Solutions. "We believe this software will redefine how businesses operate, ultimately contributing to increased profitability and sustainability."

Key Features of OptiStream:
- Predictive analytics for enhanced decision-making
- Real-time monitoring and alerts
- Seamless integration with existing systems

Availability and Demo

OptiStream is now available for businesses seeking to revolutionize their operations. To experience the power of AI-driven optimization, interested parties can request a live demo by visiting [website link].

About InnoTech Solutions

InnoTech Solutions is a forward-thinking tech start-up specializing in AI-driven

---

solutions for operational excellence. With a mission to simplify complexity, the company is committed to empowering businesses for a digitalized future.

For media inquiries, please contact:

John Doe

Media Relations Manager

Phone: [Phone Number]

E-mail: [E-mail Address]

This press release is effective in the following ways:

- **Headline:** The headline is concise, attention-grabbing, and encapsulates the main news.

- **Opening Paragraph:** The first paragraph answers the 5Ws (who, what, when, where, and why), setting the context and importance of the news.

- **Quotes:** The CEO's quote adds credibility and humanizes the announcement.

- **Key Features:** Bullet points make it easy to understand the software's benefits.

- **Availability and Demo:** Providing a call-to-action invites readers to learn more.

- **About InnoTech Solutions:** A brief background establishes the company's credibility.

- **Media Contact:** Including a media contact ensures journalists can get further information.

Crafting a well-structured press release like this ensures that the announcement is clear, informative, and ready to be shared with the media and the public.

7.3.4 Managing Crises

Effective crisis communication requires preparations and clear strategies. It is vital to address the issue with transparency, providing an honest and prompt acknowledgment of the situation. The communication should include a clear outline of the action steps the organization is taking to address and resolve the crisis. Additionally, if the situation warrants, issuing a sincere apology is a necessary step to demonstrate accountability and begin the process of rebuilding trust.

An effective crisis communication should include:

- **Transparency:** Addressing the issue honestly and promptly.

- **Action Steps:** Outlining the steps being taken to resolve the crisis.

- **Apology:** If applicable, offer a sincere apology.

Company: GlobalAirways—a leading airline carrier

Crisis Response: For Immediate Release

GlobalAirways Addresses Recent Service Disruption and Takes Steps to Ensure Customer Confidence

[City, Date]—GlobalAirways, a trusted name in air travel, acknowledges the recent service disruption experienced by some of our valued passengers. We deeply regret the inconvenience caused and are committed to resolving the issue swiftly and transparently.

Immediate Action Taken

Upon identifying the root cause of the disruption, our technical teams have worked around the clock to rectify the issue and prevent its recurrence. We have also initiated thorough inspections and safety checks to ensure the well-being of our passengers.

Committed to Customer Satisfaction

"At GlobalAirways, customer satisfaction remains our top priority. We understand the frustration caused by the recent disruption and extend our sincerest apologies to our passengers," said Emily Roberts, CEO of GlobalAirways. "We are dedicated to learning from this experience and implementing measures to enhance our service reliability."

Refund and Compensation

Passengers directly affected by the disruption will be provided full refunds and compensation as a token of our commitment to making things right. Our customer service team is actively reaching out to affected individuals to facilitate this process.

Transparency and Communication

We believe in transparency and will continue to provide regular updates on the situation as it unfolds. Our passengers can expect open communication channels, ensuring they are informed every step of the way.

Contact Information

For passengers seeking further information or assistance, our dedicated customer support team is available around the clock at [Phone Number] and [E-mail Address].

This crisis communication is effective in the following ways:

- **Acknowledgment:** The response acknowledges the issue and expresses regret for the inconvenience.

- **Immediate Action:** The response outlines the steps taken to address the problem.

- **CEO's Statement:** The CEO's statement demonstrates accountability and commitment to improvement.

- **Refund and Compensation:** Offering refunds and compensation shows the brand's dedication to customer satisfaction.

- **Transparency and Communication:** The response promises open communication and updates.

- **Contact Information:** Providing contact details ensures affected individuals can seek assistance.

Responding to a crisis with transparency, accountability, and swift action can help mitigate damage to the brand's reputation and rebuild customer trust. Effective crisis management shows a commitment to rectifying issues and demonstrates the brand's values in challenging situations.

Class Activity 12: *Read the following two articles related to corporate apologies and product recall and analyze the public relations strategies used. Write a brief report on what strategies were used, why they were chosen, and evaluate their effectiveness.*

Article 1: 10 Powerful Examples of Corporate Apologies

The two most powerful words to come out of a CEO's mouth can also be the most humbling: "I'm sorry."

When done well, corporate apologies can fix a public relations disaster and turn around it. However, when done poorly, apologies can add to the problem and seem disingenuous and insincere.

Here are 10 examples of the most powerful corporate apologies. These examples show that an open, heartfelt apology can make all the difference.

KFC Adds Humor to a Missing Chicken Situation

When KFC ran out of its most important ingredient—chicken—and had to temporarily shut down its 900 restaurants in the U.K., angry customers took to social media. KFC took a risk by adding humor to its apology in a masterful and self-deprecating way. It took out a full-page ad in London newspapers that simply showed its signature chicken bucket with a re-worked logo: "FCK." Paired with a brief explanation of the problem and a vow that it wouldn't happen again, KFC saved its brand—and its chicken.

PwC Keeps I Short After Oscars Fiasco

It was the mistake seen around the world: The wrong movie was announced as the Best Picture winner at the 2017 Oscars. Responsible for the mistake was PwC, which was tasked with counting the votes. Instead of making excuses, PwC owned its mistake and offered a short and clear apology. The statement briefly explained what happened, apologized to the people involved, and was gracious in thanking the people who handled the situation. Instead of drawing out an embarrassing situation, PwC took ownership, apologized, and moved on.

O.B. Tampons Creates 10,000 Personalized Apology Videos

Perhaps one of the best ways to apologize is to sing it. In 2010, a line of O.B. tampons was abruptly taken off the shelves after supply issues, and customers were furious. O.B.'s parent company, Johnson & Johnson, sent a personalized apology song to all 65,000-plus women in the company's database with their names in the song. In all, the company made videos for 10,000 different names. Customers could easily share the video on social media, which helped O.B. turn a potential public relations disaster into a social media win.

Apple Uses Social Media to Apologize to Taylor Swift

Anyone who's heard any of her songs knows it's not a good idea to get on Taylor Swift's bad side. The singer boycotted Apple Music after the service offered three free months to customers without paying artists. Swift posted her news on Tumblr, so Apple responded on Twitter with an apology and a statement that it would change the policy and pay artists. Apple's apology stood out because it was directly to one person on a platform everyone could see.

Airbnb's Diversity Apology Takes Action

Airbnb was accused of racial profiling and discrimination in December 2015, with a Harvard paper and social media frenzy to back up the claims. Instead of running away, Airbnb proactively addressed the issue with an e-mail from the CEO to all members. The company took a stronger stance against discrimination with a new policy and followed it up with an audit and inclusion campaign.

JetBlue CEO Offers Raw Video Apology and Promises to Change

One of the worst aviation public relation disasters came when JetBlue passengers were stranded on the tarmac for 11 hours with limited updates. After the fiasco, JetBlue's CEO shared a raw video with his apology. He also made detailed promises about how the company would prevent similar issues from happening in the future and re-committed to the company's reputation of strong customer service with the JetBlue Customer Bill of Rights.

Netflix Recognizes Not All Ideas Are Good

Back when DVDs were still an important part of Netflix's business, the company broke into two categories with separate pricing and billing—one for streaming and one for billing. The change meant a price increase that customers weren't happy about. The CEO was open and honest about the mistake and admitted he had messed up. His open letter to customers did the trick, and people appreciated that he owned the mistake.

Sony Helps Remedy Data Breach

In 2011, Sony was the victim of one of the largest data breaches in history when the personal information of 77 million PlayStation users was leaked. The CEO apologized personally and acknowledged the frustration the breach had caused. Even better, customers were given a free month of PlayStation Plus and identity theft insurance to remedy the situation.

Toyota Makes Personal Apology Visible

Toyota's biggest nightmare happened in 2010, when more than eight million cars were recalled and nearly 90 people were killed because of accidents caused by the defects. The CEO offered personal condolences to the families and emotionally apologized to all customers. To make sure everyone got the message, Toyota created an ad campaign admitting it hadn't lived up to its safety standards and took out ads in major newspapers about how it would fix the safety issues.

Domino Responds to Prank Video with Apology Video

Companies learned the danger of social media in 2009 when a video of Domino's employees putting cheese up their nose and farting on the salami they used on a customer's pizza went viral. In a respond to the prank video, Domino's CEO responded with a heartfelt apology video of his own. His video put a face to the company and outlined the company's cleanliness standards.

Every situation and apology is different, but these examples show that an honest and timely response can turn a situation around. When it comes to apologizing, taking ownership and fixing the problem goes a long way.

Article 2: Brand Reputation: Good and Bad Ways to Manage Product Recall

Hardly a month seems to go by without a brand being exposed for unsafe or fraudulent practices instigating a product recall. Volkswagen's admission in September that it sold diesel-powered cars that intentionally faked emission tests has left consumers, investors, and the media alike wanting answers.

Nestlé-owned Maggi instant noodles, meanwhile, were pulled from shelves across India earlier this year over allegations of lead levels, while Toyota last year agreed to a settlement of US $1.2 billion, concluding a four-year criminal investigation into how the carmaker handled product recalls linked to unintended acceleration.

Brands suffer two main types of damage in these situations—financial and reputational. The immediate financial impact of the recall process and any lawsuits that accompany it is typically quite high. The hit to a brand's reputation can drive that cost even higher.

"Although brands can't avoid the initial financial hit once a mistake necessitating a recall has occurred, they can greatly mitigate the reputation damage with a solid response," says Erik Bernstein, vice president of consultancy Bernstein Crisis Management.

"In Volkswagen's case, its strategy of slowly letting information out while maintaining a veil of secrecy at the top is bound to incur greater financial and reputational damage than if it had come out with complete honesty from the start."

Consumers' perception in light of a product recall can vary and has much to do with any emotional connection they may have to the brand. Zayn Khan, chief executive, Southeast Asia at brand consultancy Dragon Rouge, says that although he is disappointed in Volkswagen, he would still buy the brand and its associated marques.

"I have an emotional connection to the brands and admire their track record for innovation and aesthetics," he says. "My parents' first car was a VW Beetle, mine an Audi... Therein lies the power of the brand. It resides in a non-rational area of the brain that is sometimes blind to reason or better judgment."

The fallout from recalls can often be wider, however, if they affect other brands of the company, but this very much depends on how clear consumers are on the connection between brands and the nature of the fault. Unless the recall has some sort of crossover into the other brands, or people are very aware of the connection, related brands often go unscathed.

If the recall affects the entire product range, or if the brand is used across multiple products, the impact is likely to be considerable.

This is more evident in food categories, maintains Samir Dixit, managing director at Brand Finance Asia-Pacific, who cites the scandal engulfing Maggi noodles in India as an example. The controversy over lead levels impacted the brand as a whole, with reports that sales of Maggi pasta alongside its noodles had plunged.

The main job then becomes handling the issue, which, says Dixit, was "reasonably botched up by Nestlé India in more ways than one".

Ultimately, a brand's biggest challenge in the face of a product recall is regaining consumer trust. While the media moves on, customer mistrust can linger for a much longer time. Sometimes the turnaround can be achieved by using good and timely PR, or a change in the manufacturing process that demonstrates to consumers that the problem has been fixed.

Spending marketing dollars unless the problem is fixed at the root cause, however, will never help, believes Dixit. "It's the effectiveness of the situation and not the communication that will work."

The best way brands can recover is to own the situation. "Brands need to prove that the underlying issue has been resolved, that they have done the right thing by hurt or affected customers and that they have invested in systems and training to prevent the problem from ever happening again," says Iain Twine, chief executive, Edelman Southeast Asia and Australasia.

It is also imperative for brands to conduct a root-and-branch review of all their other risk and issue exposures.

"Brands recovering from a product recall cannot afford to be blindsided by another issue or crisis, even if it's unrelated," adds Twine. "Nothing is more likely to undermine a brand message of 'We're back and we are better than before.'"

One thing is certain: Rebuilding a brand following a product recall takes time and effort. The process requires a long-term focus on reputation, not just the next quarter's sales figures.

7.4
Writing for Marketing

Effective marketing communication is the backbone of promoting products, services, and brands. This section will delve into the art of crafting persuasive marketing content that captivates the audience, communicates value, and drives action. Whether you're drafting compelling advertisements, designing engaging campaigns, or creating attention-grabbing taglines, mastering the principles of marketing writing is essential for business success.

7.4.1 Understanding Your Audience

Identify your target audience's needs, preferences, and pain points, such as:

- Demographics, including age, gender, location, occupation, etc.
- Psychographics, including interests, values, lifestyle, behavior, etc.

Here is an example from 111SKIN about its understanding of the audience.

111SKIN is a luxury skincare brand that merges medical science with cosmetic formulations, created by Dr. Yannis Alexandrides, a renowned Harley Street cosmetic surgeon. The brand's products are designed for those seeking high-performance skincare solutions that offer clinical-level results at home. The following is an analysis of the target audience's needs, preferences, and pain points based on the brand's positioning, product range, and general market trends in luxury skincare.

Target Audience's Needs

Efficacy: Customers are looking for products that deliver visible and tangible results. They value formulations that can address specific skin concerns effectively, such as aging, hydration, brightness, and protection against environmental damage.

Quality and Safety: There's a high demand for products made with high-quality, safe ingredients. The audience prefer skincare backed by scientific research and possibly endorsed by medical professionals.

Luxury Experience: Beyond efficacy, the brand's clientele seeks a luxury experience. This includes premium packaging, texture, and scent, which makes the skincare routine enjoyable and indulgent.

Preferences

Exclusive Formulations: The target audience prefer products that contain unique, advanced, or patented ingredients that aren't readily available in mainstream skincare lines.

Professional Endorsement: Products recommended or created by dermatologists, aestheticians, or cosmetic surgeons are highly valued, as they offer a sense of trust and authority.

Sustainability: While luxury is key, there's a growing preference for brands that also consider sustainability in their packaging and sourcing of ingredients.

Pain Points

High Price Point: One of the main pain points could be the high cost associated with luxury skincare products. Customers are willing to invest in high-quality skincare but still seek justification for the price in terms of results and overall product experience.

Overwhelming Choices: The abundance of skincare products and brands can overwhelm consumers. They may find it challenging to navigate the myriad options and identify which products are truly beneficial for their specific skin concerns.

Sensitive Skin Reactions: As with any skincare brand, there's always the concern of products causing adverse reactions, particularly for those with sensitive skin. Customers are cautious about trying new products due to potential irritations or allergies.

Skepticism About Efficacy: Given the investment, there's skepticism about whether luxury skincare offers superior benefits compared to less expensive alternatives. Customers are wary of marketing claims and seek genuine proof of effectiveness.

Understanding these needs, preferences, and pain points is crucial for 111SKIN to tailor its marketing, product development, and customer service strategies effectively. The brand likely addresses these aspects by highlighting the scientific basis of its formulations, showcasing endorsements from professionals, offering detailed product information and testimonials, and perhaps providing guidance to help customers choose the right products for their skin type and concerns.

7.4.2 Crafting Compelling Headlines

In the realm of marketing, the headline is arguably the most critical element of any piece of content. Whether for an article, an advertisement, a press release, or a social media post, a compelling headline can be the difference between a message that resonates and one that is overlooked. Here's how to craft headlines that capture your audience's attention and encourage their further engagement.

1. Understanding Your Audience

Start by knowing who your audience are. A headline should speak directly to the audience's interests, needs, or problems. Understanding your audience allows you to use language and themes that resonate with them personally.

2. Keeping It Concise and Clear

A headline should be succinct yet informative. Aim for clarity over cleverness; your audience should understand the value of your content at a glance. Avoid jargon and overly complex language that might confuse or alienate them.

3. Using Actionable Language

Incorporate verbs that inspire action or evoke a sense of urgency. Words like "discover", "transform", and "learn" can motivate your audience to engage with your content. An active voice is more direct and dynamic, making your message more compelling.

4. Highlighting the Benefit

Your headline should make it clear what your audience will gain by engaging with your content. Whether it's a solution to a problem, valuable insights, or entertainment, the benefit should be front and center.

5. Leveraging Curiosity and Intrigue

Crafting headlines that pique curiosity can be highly effective. Pose a compelling question or present a surprising fact to make your audience want to delve deeper. However, ensure that your content delivers on the promise of the headline to maintain trust.

6. Using Numbers and Lists

Headlines that include numbers or imply a list (e.g., 5 Ways to Improve Your Morning Routine) often perform well because they suggest the content is structured and digestible. They set clear expectations for the audience.

7. Testing and Refining

The effectiveness of headlines can vary widely among different audiences and contexts. Use A/B testing on your website, in e-mail campaigns, or on social media to see which headlines resonate the most. Use this data to refine your approach over time.

8. Incorporating Keywords

For online content, including relevant keywords in your headline can improve search engine optimization, making it easier for your target audience to find your content. However, ensure the keywords fit naturally and do not compromise the headline's readability or appeal.

Crafting compelling headlines is both an art and a science. It requires creativity, a deep understanding of your audience, and an ongoing willingness to test and adapt. By following these guidelines, you can create headlines that not only draw your audience's attention but also encourage their deeper engagement with your content, ultimately supporting your broader marketing goals.

The following are some attention-grabbing headlines for the organic cleaning products of EcoClean:

- Discover a Cleaner, Greener Home with EcoClean's Organic Cleaning Products!
- Elevate Your Cleaning Routine with Eco-friendly Efficacy and Earth-Friendly Ingredients!
- Banish Harmful Chemicals and Embrace Nature's Power with EcoClean's Organic Cleaners!
- Cleaning with a Conscience: Introducing EcoClean's Chemical-Free Cleaning Solutions!
- Experience the Sparkle of a Safer Home with EcoClean's Eco-friendly Cleaning Line!

These headlines are effective in the following ways:

- **Message Clarity:** Each headline clearly communicates the products' essence.
- **Emotional Appeal:** Words like "greener", "eco-friendly", and "conscience" evoke positive emotions.
- **Benefit Highlight:** These headlines emphasize the benefits of using the products.
- **Curiosity:** These headlines provoke curiosity by offering a solution without revealing all details.
- **Value Proposition:** These headlines showcase the products' unique selling points.

Crafting attention-grabbing headlines for EcoClean not only captures the audience's attention but also communicates its products' eco-friendly and effective attributes. A compelling headline sparks the audience's interest and entices them to explore further, increasing the likelihood of engagement and conversions.

The press release below hits the mark in this respect. It is clear and concise. By only reading the headline, the audience immediately know the advantages of the new golf ball. Most importantly, the brand's unique selling points appear in the headline. So if the audience decide to click away from the news without reading further, the message has still effectively been delivered.

Class Activity 13: *Write a catchy headline for each product or service listed below to make an advertisement*

1. Eco-friendly reusable water bottle

2. Smartphone with advanced camera features

3. Online language learning platform

4. High-protein vegan snack bar

5. All-weather hiking boots

6. Subscription-based meal prep delivery service

7. Wireless noise-canceling headphones

8. Organic skincare line

7.4.3　Building Persuasive Copy

Writing persuasive copy is a foundational skill in marketing, aiming to influence the audience's belief or behavior and encourage them to take a desired action, such as making a purchase, signing up for a newsletter, or engaging with a brand. Effective persuasive copywriting combines psychological insights with the clear, compelling language to create a connection with the audience and motivate them towards a specific goal. Here's how to craft persuasive marketing copy.

1. Understanding Your Audience

Begin with a deep understanding of your audience. Know their desires, challenges, fears, and pain points. Persuasive copy speaks up directly for these aspects, offering solutions or improvements that resonate on a personal level.

2. Emphasizing Benefits over Features

Focus on how your product or service improves lives or solves problems. While features are important, benefits create an emotional connection by showing the audience the real value they'll receive. For example, instead of highlighting a smartphone's technical specifications, emphasize how it simplifies communication, enhances photography experience, or supports productivity.

3. Using Emotional Triggers

Emotions are powerful motivators. Whether it's joy, fear, excitement, or a sense of belonging, tapping into emotions can drive action. Craft your message to evoke specific feelings that align with your call to action.

4. Creating a Sense of Urgency

Encourage immediate action by creating a sense of urgency. Limited-time offers, exclusive deals, and low-stock alerts prompt the audience to act quickly to avoid any missing out. However, ensure that this urgency is genuine to maintain trust.

5. Leveraging Social Proof

Incorporate testimonials, reviews, endorsements, or case studies to build credibility and trust. Knowing that others have had positive experiences significantly influences the audience's decision-making processes.

6. Using a Clear, Action-Oriented Language

Be direct with your call to action. Tell your audience exactly what you want them to do next, using a clear, imperative language like "Buy Now", "Sign Up Today", or "Start Your Free Trial".

7. Simplifying Your Message

Keep your copy concise and accessible. Avoid jargon or overly complex language that might confuse or deter your audience. The easier it is to understand the value proposition and desired action, the more persuasive your copy will be.

8. Telling a Story

Stories are inherently persuasive and memorable. They can illustrate the benefits of your product or service in a relatable way, making the abstract tangible. Use storytelling to take your audience on a journey, highlighting before and after scenarios, or imagining a future where their needs are met.

9. Testing and Optimizing

Persuasive copywriting is not a one-size-fits-all approach. What works for one target audience may not work for another. Regularly test different messages, structures, and calls to action to see what resonates best and continually refine your copy based on data and feedback.

Building persuasive copy is about more than just selling a product or service; it's about creating a narrative that aligns with the audience's values and needs, evoking emotions, and compelling them to take action. By understanding your audience deeply, focusing on benefits, evoking emotions, and clearly stating the desired action, you can craft copy that not only persuades but also builds lasting relationships with your audience.

The following is an example of persuasive copy.

Product: FitFlex Gym Memberships—premium fitness experience

Unlock a Healthier, Stronger You with FitFlex Gym Memberships!

At FitFlex, we understand that your journey to fitness is unique. That's why our premium gym memberships offer more than just access to the state-of-the-art equipment. We're dedicated to empowering you to achieve your fitness goals, one milestone at a time.

Problem and Solution:

☐ Problem: Busy schedules and conflicting commitments make consistent workouts a challenge.

☐ Solution: FitFlex offers flexible hours and tailored fitness plans to accommodate your lifestyle.

Benefits:

☐ Experience a Personalized Approach: Our certified trainers craft customized workout plans based on your goals.

☐ Access to Expert Guidance: Enjoy one-on-one sessions with trainers who are passionate about your progress.

☐ Holistic Wellness: Join our fitness classes, yoga sessions, and nutrition workshops for a balanced lifestyle.

Social Proof:

☐ Donna's Success Story: "Thanks to FitFlex, I've not only lost weight but gained confidence. The trainers are my biggest cheerleaders!"

Join the FitFlex Community Today:

Your fitness journey begins here. Experience the support, guidance, and camaraderie of our FitFlex community. Choose FitFlex and make every rep count!

The copy above is persuasive in the following ways:

- **Problem and Solution:** The copy identifies common fitness obstacles and offers solutions.

- **Benefits:** The copy highlights the personalized approach, expert guidance, and holistic wellness.

- **Social Proof:** The copy shares a success story that reinforces the benefits.

- **Call to Action:** The copy encourages its readers to take immediate action and join the community.

By building persuasive copy, FitFlex Gym Memberships effectively communicates its value proposition, addressing potential challenges, showcasing benefits, and inspiring its audience to take the next step in their fitness journey.

7.4.4 Crafting Effective Calls to Action

Crafting effective calls to action is a crucial element of marketing writing that directly influences conversion rates and goal achievements. A CTA is a clear instruction to the audience, encouraging them to take a specific action that aligns with the marketing objectives, such as purchasing a product, signing up for a newsletter, or following a social media account. Here's how to create CTAs that motivate and engage your audience.

1. Being Clear and Concise

The language of your CTAs should be straightforward and to the point. Avoid ambiguity; your audience should understand exactly what action you're asking them to take. Phrases like "Buy Now", "Subscribe Today", or "Learn More" are direct and leave no room for confusion.

2. Using Action-Oriented Verbs

Start your CTAs with a verb that compels action, such as "download", "register", "call", or "visit". This approach creates a sense of urgency and prompts the audience to act.

3. Creating a Sense of Urgency

Incorporating a sense of urgency or scarcity can significantly increase the effectiveness of your CTAs. Use time-sensitive language like "offer ends soon", "limited availability", or "act now" to encourage immediate action.

4. Highlighting the Value or Benefit

Clearly articulate the benefit the user will receive by taking the action. Whether it's access to exclusive content, a free trial, or a discount, make sure the value is front and center in your CTAs. This not only incentivizes action but also aligns with the user's interests.

5. Making It Visually Standout

For digital content, the design of the CTA button or link should make it visually prominent on the page. Use contrasting colors, ample whitespace, and a size that is large enough to be noticed without overwhelming the rest of the content.

6. Placing CTAs Strategically

Position your CTAs where they are most likely to catch attention and drive action. This could be at the end of a compelling piece of content, within the body of a blog post where relevant, or at a pivotal point on your website.

7. Personalizing When Possible

Tailoring the CTA to the user's interests or past behavior can increase its effectiveness. Use data and insights to customize the CTA for different segments of your audience.

8. Testing and Optimizing

Continuously test different versions of your CTAs to determine what works best. Experiment with different verbs, formats, colors, and placements. Use the A/B testing to measure performance and refine your approach based on data.

9. Providing Assurance

If the action involves a commitment, like signing up or making a purchase, alleviate potential concerns with reassurances such as "no credit card required", "unsubscribe at any time", or "secure checkout".

An effective CTA is much more than just a button or a line of text; it's a crucial component of your marketing strategy that guides users towards your desired outcomes. By making your CTAs clear, compelling, and easy to find, you can enhance user engagement, improve conversion rates, and ultimately achieve your marketing goals. Crafting a powerful CTA requires understanding your audience, offering value, and continuously refining your approach based on performance insights.

The following are some examples of effective calls to action.

> Campaign:"StayBright Dental Clinic"—providing teeth whitening services
> - Ready to Shine Bright? Book Your Teeth Whitening Session Today!
> - Claim Your Confident Smile: Schedule Your Teeth Whitening Appointment Now!
> - Experience Radiant Results: Reserve Your Teeth Whitening Treatment!
> - Unlock Your Best Smile: Secure Your Teeth Whitening Spot!
> - Say Hello to a Brighter You: Book Your Teeth Whitening Session!

These CTAs are effective in the following ways:

- **Clear and Direct:** The CTAs convey a specific action the audience should take.

- **Urgency:** Words like "Today", "Now", and "Reserve" create a sense of urgency.

- **Value Proposition:** The CTAs promise positive outcomes ("Shine Bright", "Confident Smile", "Radiant Results").

- **Emotion:** Phrases like "Unlock Your Best Smile" and "Say Hello to a Brighter You" evoke positive emotions.

- **Benefit Emphasis:** The CTAs focus on the benefit of the action, motivating the audience to engage.

Crafting effective CTAs for StayBright Dental Clinic encourages the audience to take immediate action and book teeth whitening services. By using persuasive language, urgency, and value-driven messages, these CTAs drive engagement and conversions, leading to increased appointments and a brighter, more confident clientele.

7.4.5 Creating Visual Impact

In the digital age, creating a strong visual impact is as crucial as the written content in your marketing efforts. Visuals catch the eye, convey emotions, and can significantly increase engagement and recall of your messages. Here's how to integrate compelling visuals into your marketing strategies to complement your writing and maximize impact.

1. **Understanding the Power of Visuals**

   Visuals can communicate complex information quickly, evoke emotions, and influence decisions. In a crowded digital landscape, an impactful visual can make your content stand out and be remembered.

2. **Aligning Visuals with Brand Identity**

   Ensure all visuals align with your brand identity, including colors, fonts, and style. Consistent visual branding helps build recognition and trust among your audience. It reinforces your brand's messages and values at every touchpoint.

3. **Using High-Quality Images**

   Quality matters when it comes to visuals. High-resolution images that look professional and are relevant to your content can significantly enhance the perceived value of your messages. Poor-quality images, on the other hand, can detract from your credibility.

4. **Optimizing for Different Platforms**

   Tailor your visuals for the specific requirements of each platform. Dimensions, file sizes, and formats vary across social media, e-mail, and web. Customizing visuals ensures they look their best wherever they're viewed.

5. **Incorporating Infographics and Data Visualization**

   Infographics and data visualizations turn complex information into easy-to-understand, engaging graphics. They are particularly effective for summarizing research findings, illustrating trends, or explaining how something works.

6. **Leveraging Video Content**

   Video is a powerful tool for storytelling and can increase user engagement significantly. Whether it's a product demonstration, an educational piece, or a behind-the-scenes look at your operation, video content can provide a richer, more dynamic user experience.

7. Using Visuals to Complement the Text

Visuals should complement and enhance your written messages, not replace them. Use images and graphics to break up text, illustrate points, and create a visually appealing layout that encourages the audience to keep engaging with your content.

8. Including Calls to Action in Visuals

Visual CTAs can be highly effective. Including a call to action within an image or at the end of a video can direct the audience towards the next step you want them to take, from visiting a website to making a purchase.

9. Testing and Measuring Impact

Just as with written content, it's important to test and measure the impact of your visuals. Use analytics to track how different types of visuals perform in terms of engagement, click-through rates, and conversions. This data can inform your future visual strategy.

10. Ensuring Accessibility

Make your visuals accessible to everyone, including those with visual impairments. Use alt text for images, and captions for videos, and ensure that your color choices have sufficient contrast.

Visuals are a critical component of effective marketing. They not only attract attention but also help communicate your messages more effectively, evoke emotional responses, and encourage engagement. By carefully selecting and optimizing visuals to complement your written content, you can create a more impactful and memorable marketing message. Remember, the goal is to use visuals and text in harmony to tell a compelling story that resonates with your audience and drives them towards your desired action.

The following is an example of using visuals in the marketing.

Product: TechSculpt—innovative 3D printing technology
Visual Impact:

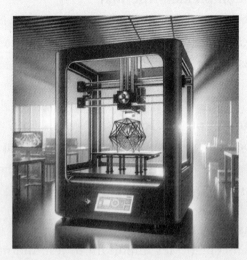

Image: A sleek, futuristic 3D printer in action, crafting intricate designs with precision

Copy:

☐ Explore the Future of Creation with TechSculpt 3D Printing!

Unleash your imagination and bring your designs to life with TechSculpt's cutting-edge 3D printing technology. From intricate prototypes to artistic masterpieces, our precision-driven printer transforms ideas into tangible reality.

☐ Precision in Every Layer:

Witness perfection in every layer as TechSculpt's advanced technology creates intricate designs with unmatched accuracy.

☐ Limitless Possibilities:

Whether you're an architect, designer, or hobbyist, TechSculpt opens a world of creative potential at your fingertips.

☐ Innovate with Ease:

Our user-friendly interface ensures seamless printing, enabling you to focus on your vision while TechSculpt brings it to life.

Ready to Shape the Future?

Join the revolution of creativity with TechSculpt 3D Printing. Explore the possibilities and craft the extraordinary!

The visual is impactful in the following ways:

- **Compelling Visual:** The image showcases the product in action, adding visual context.

- **Clear and Engaging Copy:** The copy complements the image, explaining benefits succinctly.

- **Highlighting Features:** Bullet points emphasize key features for quick understanding.

- **Emphasis on Imagination:** The copy encourages the audience to imagine their creation.

- **Call to Action:** The CTA invites the audience to be part of the revolutionary journey.

By combining captivating visuals with engaging copy, TechSculpt communicates the essence of its product and showcases its potential to readers. This approach not only captures the audience's attention but also effectively communicates the product's features and benefits, inspiring them to explore the possibilities of 3D printing.

7.4.6　Utilizing Storytelling

Storytelling is a powerful tool in marketing, capable of transforming how the audience perceive, connect with, and remember your brand. It moves beyond mere facts and figures, weaving them into narratives that evoke emotion, build relationships, and inspire action. Here's how to effectively incorporate storytelling into your marketing strategies.

1. **Embracing the Core Elements of Storytelling**

   Characters: Introduce relatable characters that your audience can connect with. This could be a customer, an employee, or the brand itself personified.

   Conflict: Present a problem or challenge that your character faces, aligning it with common pain points or desires of your target audience.

   Resolution: Showcase how your product or service provides a solution, transforming the character's situation and offering a satisfying conclusion.

2. **Connecting on an Emotional Level**

   Utilize emotions to create a bond between your audience and your story. Whether it's joy, surprise, empathy, or aspiration, emotional engagement makes your messages more memorable and impactful.

3. Aligning Stories with Brand Values

Ensure your stories reflect and reinforce your brand's core values. This consistency strengthens your brand identity and fosters trust and loyalty among your audience.

4. Using Authenticity to Build Trust

Authentic stories resonate more deeply with the audience. Share real experiences, customer testimonials, or behind-the-scenes glimpses into your brand. Authenticity enhances credibility and encourages your audience to invest emotionally in your narrative.

5. Crafting Stories for Different Platforms

Tailor your storytelling to fit the format and audience of each platform, from long-form articles and blog posts to short videos on social media. Consider the unique features and user behavior of each platform to maximize engagement.

6. Incorporating Visual and Sensory Elements

Enhance your stories with visuals, sounds, and other sensory details to make them more vivid and engaging. Multimedia elements can help bring your story to life, making it more immersive and effective.

7. Encouraging User Participation

Invite your audience to share their own stories related to your brand or product. User-generated content can provide authentic narratives that resonate with your wider audience and deepen community engagement.

8. Highlighting the Journey

Focus on the journey, not just the outcome. Showing the process of transformation or overcoming challenges can be more compelling than simply presenting results. It provides depth to the narrative and can inspire your audience to envision their own journey with your brand.

9. Measuring and Adapting

Track the effectiveness of your storytelling efforts through engagement metrics, feedback, and conversion rates. Use these insights to refine your approach and better align your stories with audience preferences and behavior.

Storytelling in marketing is about more than just selling a product or service; it's about creating meaningful connections with your audience. By crafting engaging narratives that resonate on an emotional level, you can elevate your brand, differentiate from competitors, and drive powerful engagement. Remember, the best stories are those that not only tell but also show, creating an experience that stays with the audience long after they've engaged with your content.

The following is an example of storytelling in the marketing.

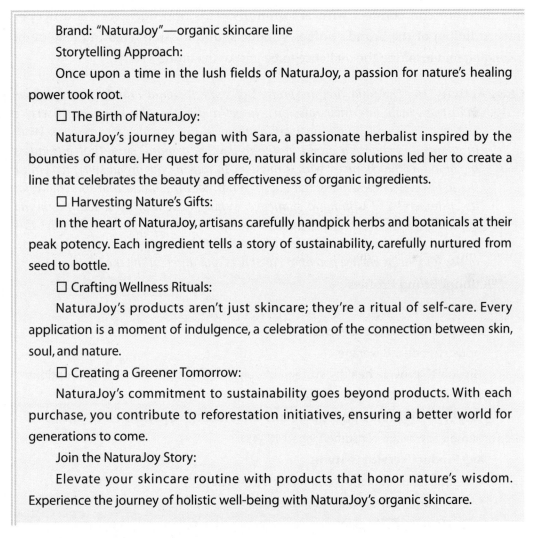

Brand: "NaturaJoy"—organic skincare line

Storytelling Approach:

Once upon a time in the lush fields of NaturaJoy, a passion for nature's healing power took root.

☐ The Birth of NaturaJoy:

NaturaJoy's journey began with Sara, a passionate herbalist inspired by the bounties of nature. Her quest for pure, natural skincare solutions led her to create a line that celebrates the beauty and effectiveness of organic ingredients.

☐ Harvesting Nature's Gifts:

In the heart of NaturaJoy, artisans carefully handpick herbs and botanicals at their peak potency. Each ingredient tells a story of sustainability, carefully nurtured from seed to bottle.

☐ Crafting Wellness Rituals:

NaturaJoy's products aren't just skincare; they're a ritual of self-care. Every application is a moment of indulgence, a celebration of the connection between skin, soul, and nature.

☐ Creating a Greener Tomorrow:

NaturaJoy's commitment to sustainability goes beyond products. With each purchase, you contribute to reforestation initiatives, ensuring a better world for generations to come.

Join the NaturaJoy Story:

Elevate your skincare routine with products that honor nature's wisdom. Experience the journey of holistic well-being with NaturaJoy's organic skincare.

The storytelling is effective in the following ways:

- **Emotional Connection:** The storytelling approach evokes emotions and engages the audience.

- **Brand Values:** The story aligns with the brand's commitment to nature and sustainability.

- **Visual Imagery:** The narrative paints vivid imagery of the brand's origins and processes.

- **Creating Identity:** The story creates an identity that the audience can resonate with.

- **Call to Action:** The CTA invites the audience to be part of the brand's journey.

Utilizing storytelling, NaturaJoy transforms its brand into a narrative that the audience can connect with emotionally. This approach fosters a deeper understanding of the brand's values, products, and mission, creating a sense of belonging and inspiring the audience to be part of the brand's story.

Class Activity 14: *The following are profiles of some fictional brands across various industries, including their missions, target audiences, and key product/service features. The storytelling framework handout is also provided for reference. Work in groups and choose a brand profile to develop a brand story that introduces the brand as the character with a mission. In making the brand story, remember the following: 1) Describing the quest: What does the brand aim to achieve for its customers? 2) Outlining a challenge: What problem or need does the brand address? 3) Offering a resolution: How does the brand's product/service solve this problem? Then present the brand story to the class, discussing how each element of the story helps engage potential customers and differentiate the brand.*

Fictional Brand Profiles

Brand 1: GreenSprout Foods

Industry: Food & Beverage

Mission: to provide healthy, sustainable, and delicious plant-based food options for environmentally conscious consumers.

Target Audience: health-conscious individuals, vegetarians, vegans, and environmentally-aware consumers, aged 18–45.

Key Product/Service Features:

- A wide range of plant-based meals and snacks;
- Use of organic, non-GMO ingredients;
- Eco-friendly packaging.

Brand 2: TechTrend

Industry: Consumer Electronics

Mission: to innovate everyday life with cutting-edge technology that's accessible to everyone.

Target Audience: tech enthusiasts and the general public seeking the latest gadgets, aged 20–50.

Key Product/Service Features:

- Smart home devices that integrate seamlessly;
- User-friendly interface and design;
- Affordable pricing without compromising on quality.

Brand 3: ZenSpace Interiors

Industry: Home Decor and Furniture

Mission: to transform homes into tranquil sanctuaries with beautifully designed, minimalist furniture and decor.

Target Audience: homeowners and renters looking for modern, minimalist interior design solutions, aged 25–60.

Key Product/Service Features:

- Minimalist furniture with sustainable materials;
- Home decor consultation services;
- Online visualization tools for interior planning.

Brand 4: Wanderlove Apparel

Industry: Fashion and Apparel

Mission: to inspire adventure and love for the outdoors through eco-friendly and stylish outdoor apparel.

Target Audience: outdoor enthusiasts, travelers, and fashion-forward consumers who value sustainability, aged 18–40.

Key Product/Service Features:

- Durable, weather-resistant clothing made from recycled materials;
- A portion of proceeds goes to environmental conservation efforts;
- Trendy designs that transition from outdoor activities to casual wear.

Brand 5: Paws & Reflect Pet Care

Industry: Pet Products and Services

Mission: to enhance the well-being of pets and their owners through innovative, compassionate, and eco-friendly products and services.

Target Audience: pet owners who treat their pets as family and are committed to their health and happiness, aged 20–60.

Key Product/Service Features:

- Organic pet food and eco-friendly toys;

- Mobile vet and grooming services;
- Community events for pets and their owners.

Storytelling Framework Handout

The Four Key Elements of a Story
- Character: Introduce the protagonist of your story. In a brand story, this could be the brand itself, a customer, or a character representing your target audience.
- Quest: What is the goal or mission? For brands, this often involves solving a problem or fulfilling a need for the target audience.
- Challenge: Describe the obstacles or challenges faced along the way. This could be a common problem your target audience encounter that your product/service needs to address.
- Resolution: How does the story end? Show how the character overcomes the challenge, ideally through the use of your product/service, and what the outcome is.

Tips for Effective Storytelling
- Relating to Your Audience: Craft stories that resonate with the emotions, desires, and needs of your target audience.
- Being Authentic: Authenticity strengthens trust. Ensure your stories reflect your brand's values and mission.
- Incorporate Visuals: When possible, use visuals to complement your narrative, making it more engaging and memorable.
- Call to Action: Conclude your story with a call to action that encourages your audience to engage further with your brand.

7.4.7 Maximizing Digital Platforms

In the dynamic landscape of digital marketing, leveraging a variety of platforms effectively is key to reaching and engaging with your target audience. Each platform offers unique opportunities to connect with users, share content, and drive conversions. Here's how to maximize the potential of digital platforms in your marketing strategies.

1. Identifying the Right Platforms

Audience Alignment: Choose the platforms where your target audience is most active. Conduct market research to understand the demographics and behavior of users on different platforms.

Brand Compatibility: Select the platforms that align with your brand's voice and content style. Visual brands might prioritize Instagram, while B2B companies may find more values in LinkedIn.

2. Tailoring Content for Each Platform

Platform-Specific Content: Adapt your content to fit the format, norms, and user expectations of each platform. What works on X might not resonate on Facebook or Instagram.

Optimize for Engagement: Use platform-specific features to enhance engagement. This could include stories on Instagram, live videos on Facebook, or polls and threads on X.

3. Utilizing SEO and SEM Strategies

Search Engine Optimization (SEO): Optimize your website and content for search engines to improve visibility in search results. Use relevant keywords, meta tags, and quality backlinks.

Search Engine Marketing (SEM): Leverage paid advertising options on search engines and social platforms to increase visibility and drive targeted traffic to your site.

4. Engaging in Social Listening and Monitoring

Track Mentions: Use tools to monitor mentions of your brand, products, or industry keywords. This can provide insights into audience sentiment, emerging trends, and opportunities for engagement.

Respond and Interact: Actively respond to comments, messages, and mentions. Engaging with users can build relationships and foster a positive brand image.

5. Analyzing and Leveraging Data

Analytics Tools: Utilize the analytics tools provided by each platform to track the performance of your content. Look at metrics like reach, engagement, click-through rates, and conversions.

Data-Driven Decisions: Use the insights gained from analytics to inform your strategy. Test different types of content, posting times, and campaigns to see what yields the best results.

6. Integrating Across Channels

Cross-Promotion: Promote your content across different platforms to maximize reach. For example, share your blog posts on social media or include social links in your e-mail newsletters.

Consistent Messaging: Ensure that your brand messages are consistent across all digital platforms, though tailored to fit each platform's unique style.

7. Fostering Community and User Engagement

Build Relationships: Use digital platforms to build a community around your brand. Encourage user-generated content, run contests, and create interactive campaigns that invite participation.

Value Exchange: Provide values for your audience through informative, entertaining, or inspirational content. This helps keep users engaged and loyal to your brand.

Maximizing digital platforms requires a strategic approach tailored to the strengths and audience of each platform. By understanding where your audience spend their time and how they engage with content, you can craft a digital marketing strategy that leverages the full potential of these platforms. Remember, the key to success is not just presence, but active engagement, consistent messaging, and a deep understanding of data-driven insights to continually refine and improve your approach.

The following is an example of maximizing digital platforms.

Company: TastyBites—gourmet food delivery service
Optimized Social Media Post:
- Instagram Post:

Craving gourmet goodness? Look no further! Indulge in our chef-crafted dishes, delivered to your doorstep. From succulent burgers to divine desserts, we've got your cravings covered. Order now and treat yourself to a #TastyBites experience!
- Website Homepage Banner:

Banner Image: A tantalizing spread of TastyBites' gourmet dishes.
Copy:
Elevate Your Culinary Experience: Order Gourmet Delights from TastyBites Today!
Savor the essence of exquisite flavors with TastyBites. Our culinary artisans blend passion with premium ingredients to create a symphony of taste that delights your palate. Explore our menu and embark on a gastronomic journey like no other.

- Facebook Ad:

Ad Visual: A vibrant image showcasing TastyBites' diverse range of dishes.

Copy:

Experience Culinary Magic: Order Now and Delight in Gourmet Feasts!

From intimate dinners to special celebrations, TastyBites transforms every moment into a gourmet affair. Indulge in our signature dishes, thoughtfully crafted to satisfy even the most discerning tastes. Discover culinary excellence with TastyBites!

The example maximizes digital platforms in the following ways:

- **Tailored to Platform:** Each post is optimized for the specific platform's style and format.
- **Engaging Imagery:** Visuals showcase the delicious range of dishes, capturing the audience's attention.
- **Inviting Copy:** The copy entices the audience with appealing language and benefits.
- **Hashtags:** Utilizing relevant hashtags increases discoverability and engagement.
- **Call to Action:** The CTAs prompt the audience to take immediate action, driving conversions.

By maximizing digital platforms, TastyBites effectively promotes its gourmet food delivery service to a wider audience. Each platform-specific post engages users, communicates value, and encourages them to explore the menu and indulge in a delightful culinary experience.

Effective marketing writing goes beyond mere promotion; it's about creating connections, resonating with target audience, and inspiring action. By understanding your audience, mastering persuasive techniques, and adapting to various platforms, you'll be equipped to craft marketing messages that leave a lasting impact, foster brand loyalty, and drive business growth.

教师服务

　　感谢您选用清华大学出版社的教材！为了更好地服务教学，我们为授课教师提供本学科重点教材信息及样书，请您扫码获取。

≫ 最新书目

扫码获取 2024 **外语类** 重点教材信息

≫ 样书赠送

教师扫码即可获取样书